D1127863

𝕿𝖍𝖊 𝕾𝖎𝖑𝖛𝖊𝖗 𝕾𝖊𝖗𝖎𝖊𝖘 𝖔𝖋 𝕸𝖔𝖉𝖊𝖗𝖓 𝕷𝖆𝖓𝖌𝖚𝖆𝖌𝖊 𝕿𝖊𝖝𝖙-𝕭𝖔𝖔𝖐𝖘

EDITED BY

ADOLPHE COHN, LL.B., A.M.

PROFESSOR OF THE ROMANCE LANGUAGES AND LITERATURES IN
COLUMBIA UNIVERSITY

AN ELEMENTARY GRAMMAR

OF THE

SPANISH LANGUAGE

The Silver Series of Modern Language Text-Books

AN
ELEMENTARY GRAMMAR

OF THE

SPANISH LANGUAGE

BY

L. A. LOISEAUX, B.S.

ADJUNCT PROFESSOR OF THE ROMANCE LANGUAGES AND LITERATURES
COLUMBIA UNIVERSITY

SILVER, BURDETT AND COMPANY

NEW YORK   BOSTON   CHICAGO

Copyright, 1900,

By Silver, Burdett & Company

PREFACE

No apology need be presented for the publication of a new Spanish grammar or text-book. The growing interest of the public in the only language that can be considered a rival of the English tongue on the American continent requires the production of new and more perfect instruments for the acquisition of that language.

The present volume is to be considered a "First Spanish Book." It is intended for young people in high schools as well as colleges, who have no acquaintance as yet with the language of Lope de Vega and Cervantes, of Simon Bolivar, the liberator of South America, and Don Emilio Castelar, the glory of Spanish political oratory.

It is to be used both as an Elementary Grammar and as a practical method for the acquisition of a simple vocabulary and of the most frequent idioms of the language. It must not, therefore, be considered a complete grammar of the Spanish language. The exercises for the translation of English into Spanish have been devised with the view of suggesting to the student the most idiomatic Spanish sentence accessible to him at the stage he has reached, and to this fact must be ascribed the slight clumsiness which will here and there be discovered in the English wording.

The Grammar will be supplemented by a Reader, also due to the labors of Mr. L. A. Loiseaux, who, through his experience as an instructor of Spanish in Columbia University, has become thoroughly acquainted with the obstacles to be overcome by the American student in his struggle for the mastery of *la lengua castellana*.

ADOLPHE COHN.

CONTENTS

AN

ELEMENTARY SPANISH GRAMMAR

INTRODUCTORY

ALPHABET, PRONUNCIATION AND ACCENT

ALPHABET

1. The Spanish alphabet contains the same letters as the English, to which should be added the four compound letters: **ch, ll, ñ, rr.** These represent distinct sounds. **k** and **w,** however, are found only in foreign words.

PRONUNCIATION

2. The sound of the Spanish vowels **never** changes. It is the same as that of the Latin vowels in what is known as the Roman pronunciation. (See § 4 for the pronunciation of **e** and **o.**) The only difference to be observed is that of duration between the accented, always long, and the unaccented, always short.

The consonants are less distinctly pronounced than the vowels, being somewhat softened, and sometimes even silent.

3. While nothing can take the place of oral explanation, an approximate idea of Spanish sounds, by means of English words, is given below.

Vowels

4. a like *a* in *ah!* **plāta** *, **fanāl**.

e like *a* in *late* when ending a syllable: **pārte, nŏble**, otherwise open like *e* in *set:* **papēl, ēsta**.

i like *e* in *me:* **mil, fīla**.

o like *o* in *go*, when unaccented or ending a syllable: **mālo, lībro**; otherwise open like *o* in *come:* **dolōr, mōdo**.

u like *u* in *rude:* **plūma, ūno**.   (Silent after *g* and *q*, unless marked with diæresis (··).

y when alone or final the same as *i*.   In other cases like *y* in *year*.

5. Vowels are divided into: Strong vowels, **a, e, o**; and weak vowels, **i** (when final: *y*) and **u**.

A diphthong is formed by the combination of a strong vowel and a weak one, or of two weak vowels which must be different.   Both vowels keep their individual sound, but they are pronounced as a single syllable, a slight stress being laid in the first case on the strong vowel and in the second, on the last of the two weak vowels.

Ex.—pai–sā–no, caū–sa, prē–cio, rey, viū–do, muy.

A triphthong consists of a strong vowel between two weak ones, the combination counting as one syllable.

Ex.—a–pre–ciáis, a–pre–ciéis, buey.

Two strong vowels cannot form a diphthong, and each belongs to a distinct syllable.

Ex.—trā–e, lē–o, de–sē–o, nā–o.

When it is necessary to place the accent-mark † over a syllable containing a diphthong (or triphthong), the accent-

---

* (–) indicates accented syllable.   It should not be written.   *Cf.* § **7**, Remark (*a*).

† See § **7**, Remarks (*a*) and (*b*).

mark is placed over the strong vowel; if both vowels are weak, over the last one.

Ex.—hués–ped, mur–cié–la–go, fuí.

An accent-mark placed over the weak vowel, or over the first of two weak vowels, dissolves the diphthong (or triphthong).

Ex.—frí–o, pa–ís, flú–i–do, te–mí–ais.

Consonants

6. **f, k, l, m, n, p, w,** are pronounced as in English.

b and **v,** differ from English *b* and *v,* in that their pronunciation is almost alike. They are uttered with the lips close together but not completely touching each other. Many words are found spelled indifferently with *b* or *v,* **ex. : Habana, Havana.**

c, like *k* before *a, o, u* or a consonant; before *e* or *i,* like *th* in *think.*

ch has always the sound of *ch* in *chair.*

d like the English *d,* but slightly softer. When final, or between vowels, it sounds nearly like *th* in *although.*

g before *a, o, u* or a consonant is pronounced like *g* in *go ;* before *e* or *i,* it has the sound of *j* as below.

j has a sound almost impossible to describe in writing, that of *h* in *hate,* but more guttural and strongly aspirate. It approaches the sound of *ch* in the German *Aachen.*

h is silent everywhere, except in a very few words.

ll is pronounced like *lli* in *million.*

ñ has the sound of *ni* in *onion.* (*cf* **cañón,** canyon.)

q is equivalent to *k.* (It occurs only before *ue* and *ui.*)

r is strongly rolled when initial, less so between vowels.

rr has the sound of a prolonged *r*, both letters being distinctly pronounced.

s like *s* in *send*, never as in *rose*.

t as English *t* in *tell*.   (It retains that sound even when followed by *i* and another vowel, **ex. : pātio.**)

x like *x* in *tax*, *axe*.

z always like *th* in *thought*.   It is never found before *e* or *i*.

NOTE.—The only letters that can be doubled are *c* (before *e* or *i*), *n*, and *r*.

Tonic Accent

7. In words of two or more syllables, one syllable is pronounced with more emphasis than the others.   This emphasis in pronunciation is called **tonic accent.**

The place of the tonic accent is governed by the following rules :

The accent rests :

(1) On the last syllable :

(*a*) In words ending with a consonant other than *n* or *s* : **ciudad,** *city,* **canal,** *canal ;* (*b*) in most of the nouns ending in *n*, especially those ending in *ión*.   These bear the accent-mark (') : **jardín,** *garden,* **Alemán,** *German,* **nación,** *nation.*

(2) On the penultimate :

(*a*) In words ending with a vowel or a diphthong : **casa,** *house,* **libro,** *book ;* (*b*) in words other than nouns, ending with *n* or *s* : **aman,** *they love,* **estamos,** *we are ;* (*c*) in proper names ending in *ez* : **Gomez, Nuñez.**

(3) On the antepenultimate :

In a few words which cannot be classified.   On these words the accent-mark (') is always printed, **ex. : artículo,** *article,* **música,** *music.*

REMARKS.—(*a*) Any deviation from the above rules is indicated by an accent-mark (´) over the accented syllable. (*b*) The accent-mark is also used to distinguish words of identical forms, but of different meanings, **ex.: él,** *he,* **el,** *the,* **cómo,** *I eat,* **como,** *as.* (*c*) The addition of *s* or *es* indicating the plural never changes the place of the tonic accent (except in **carácter, régimen,** which give **caracteres, regímenes** in the plural). (*d*) In compound words, each of the component words retains its own accent.

Division of Syllables

8. Spanish words are divided in such a way that every syllable shall begin with a consonant (if possible).

Ex.—co–mi–da, a–me–ri–ca–no.

(*a*) **ch, ll, ñ, rr** are considered as simple consonants, and follow the above rule.

Ex.—co–che, ga–lli–na, ca–ñón, ca–rro.

(*b*) **l** and **r** when preceded by a consonant other than *s*, are not separated from that consonant.

Ex.—no–ble, ma–dre.

(*c*) **s** does not combine with a following consonant.

Ex.—es–ca–le–ra, es–tar.

(*d*) Vowels forming a diphthong (or triphthong) should not be separated.

Ex.—bue–no, pa–tria, rei–no, san–ti–guáis.

NOTE.—A single vowel should not end or begin a line.

EXERCISE

PRONUNCIATION AND ACCENT

A. Amo, amigo, ala; me, era, efecto; mi, visita, listo; no, dolor, corto; uno, pluma, unido; y, muy, yerba.

B. Boca, buscar, lobo, Habana ; cama, color, Cuba ; cena, cita ; chico, mucho, noche ; deber, dar, dedo, edad, Madrid ; gato, golpe, gusto, guapo, agua, sigue, seguir ; general, gesto, gitano ; mujer, ajeno, naranja, jurar, alhaja ; hablar, hijo ; calle, castillo, llave, lleno ; señor, baño, niña ; querer, queso, tranquilo ; rato, rico, pero, perro, coro, corro ; casa, es, mesa ; tal, tema, triste ; mozo, zapato, azul.

C. Baile, aire, paisano, causa, autor, cual, cuando, Juan ; veinte, reino, reinado, aceite, nadie, bien ; Europa, neutro, bueno, luego, hueso ; óleo, correo, precio, patio, tío, nación, servicio, oír, oído ; ciudad, ciudadano, cuidar, cuidado, viudo, perpetuo, virtuoso.

CHAPTER I.

THE ARTICLE

9. The article is definite or indefinite. It always agrees in gender and number with its noun.

The Definite Article

10.

	Masculine	Feminine	Neuter
Singular	el	la	lo
Plural	los	las	

Ex.—el padre, *the father.* los padres, *the fathers.*
el sombrero, *the hat.* los sombreros, *the hats.*
la madre, *the mother.* las madres, *the mothers.*
la casa, *the house.* las casas, *the houses.*

For use of *lo,* see § **14.**

11. When the prepositions **de,** *of,* and **á,** *to,* are followed immediately by the definite article **el,** preposition and article are contracted into **del** and **al** respectively.

Ex.—del padre, *of the father.* al padre, *to the father.*

12. Before a feminine singular noun beginning with accented **a** or **ha,** the masculine article **el** is used instead of the feminine **la.**

Ex.—el alma, *the soul.* but: la animación, *the stir.*
el agua, *the water.* " la alhaja, *the jewel.*
el hacha, *the axe.* " la hacienda, *the estate.*

This change is not made before a plural noun or before an adjective: **las almas,** *the souls,* **la alta casa,** *the high house.*

13. While in most cases the use of the definite article is the same in Spanish as in English, the following differences should be noted.

Spanish requires the definite article :

(*a*) Before nouns used in a general or absolute sense.

Ex.—El hombre es mortal,   *Man is mortal.*
Los perros son animales útiles,   *Dogs are useful animals.*

(*b*) Before the names of the days of the week :

Ex.—los martes y viernes,   *Tuesdays and Fridays.*

(*c*) Before titles when the person is spoken of, not when addressed.

Ex.—el señor y la señora X...,   *Mr. and Mrs. X...*
el rey Alfonso Trece,   *King Alfonso the Thirteenth.*

14. The article **lo** is used before adjectives, having an abstract meaning.

Ex.—lo bueno,   *the good, what is good.*
lo malo,   *the evil, what is evil.*

The Indefinite Article

15. *Masc.* un, *a, an,*   *Fem.* una, *a, an.*

Ex.—un hombre,   *a man.*   un libro,   *a book.*
una mujer,   *a woman.*   una pluma,   *a pen.*

16. The plural forms **unos** (*masc.*), and **unas** (*fem.*), are sometimes used with the sense of *some, a few,* . . . to express the partitive value of a noun.

Ex.—tengo unos libros muy   *I have some (a few) very pretty*
bonitos,   *books.*

17. The indefinite article is omitted in Spanish :

(*a*) Before a noun in the predicate used like an adjective to denote occupation, profession, rank, etc.

Ex.—es capitán,   *he is a captain.*
es comerciante,   *he is a merchant.*

(*b*) In several indefinite expressions :

Ex.—tal día, *such a day.* cierta cosa, *a certain thing.*
  otro papel, *another paper.*

EXERCISE I.

VOCABULARY I.

tiene, *has.* da, *gives.*

(Also words given in preceding Chapter.)

A. 1. El padre y la madre. 2. La hacienda del comerciante. 3. Tengo un libro muy útil. 4. El rey da una casa al capitán. 5. El hombre tiene un sombrero. 6. La animación de la casa. 7. Tengo libros y plumas. 8. El padre da una alhaja á la madre. 9. El comerciante tiene una casa muy bonita. 10. Una pluma es una cosa útil.

B. 1. The man and the woman. 2. Mr. X... is a merchant. 3. The estate of the King. 4. I have a book and a pen. 5. The house of Mrs. B... 6. I have the hat of the captain. 7. Man is mortal. 8. The merchant gives a house to Mr. C... 9. I have a dog. 10. The soul of the man. 11. The book is useful. 12. The good and the evil.

CHAPTER II.

NOUNS

18. Spanish nouns have no special case forms, not even a possessive case like the English, this being expressed by means of a preposition.

Ex.—*My father's house.* La casa de mi padre.

Gender

19. Spanish has only two genders: Masculine and Feminine. Every noun, whatever it represents, must be either one or the other.

Ex.—el hombre, *the man,*   la mujer, *the woman.*
el libro,   *the book* (masc.)   la pluma, *the pen* (fem.)

20. Nouns denoting males, titles or professions commonly assigned to males are **masculine**, whatever their endings. Those denoting females, professions or dignities pertaining to females are **feminine**.

Ex.—*masc.,* el juez, *the judge.*   la emperatriz, *the empress.*
masc., el cura, *the curate.*   la costurera, *the seamstress.*

This rule outweighs all others.

21. In other nouns, the ending **o** usually indicates the masculine gender, the ending **a** the feminine.

Ex.—*masc.,* el grano,   *the grain.*   *fem.,* la tinta,   *the ink.*
masc., el palacio,   *the palace.*   *fem.,* la casa,   *the house.*

22. The above rule, however, suffers many exceptions

The following remarks will help to determine the gender of nouns not included in § **20**.

Nouns which do not imply a distinction of sex are:

Masculine:

(*a*) when ending in **o** (§ **21**) except **la mano,** *the hand.*

(*b*) when ending in **–ma** (Greek and Latin derivatives), **ex.:** **el drama,** *the drama;* **el poema,** *the poem.*

Feminine:

(*a*) when ending in **a** (§ **21**) except **el día,** *the day.*

(*b*) when ending in **d,–ión,–ie, ex.: la ciudad,** *the city,* **la nación,** *the nation,* **la serie,** *the series.*

23. The names of days, months, rivers, oceans, mountains, and indeclinable parts of speech used as nouns are masculine.

Ex.—el lunes,	*Monday.*	el Rín,	*the Rhine.*
el Atlántico,	*the Atlantic.*	los Alpes,	*the Alps.*
el creer,	*believing, belief.*	el pero,	*the "but."*

24. Compound nouns are masculine when made up of a verb and a noun, otherwise they take the gender of the second part.

Ex.—el cortaplumas,	*the pen-knife.*	el mediodía,	*the mid-day.*
la sinrazón,	*the injustice.*		

25. The gender of nouns not included in the above remarks can best be learned by practice.

Ex.—*masc.,* el árbol,	*the tree.*	*fem.,* la calle,	*the street.*
masc., el sol,	*the sun.*	*fem.,* la paz,	*the peace.*

Number

26. Nouns in Spanish have two numbers, the singular and the plural.

27. The plural of nouns is formed as follows:

(1) By adding **s** to the singular if the noun ends:

(*a*) with an unaccented vowel (except **y**).

Ex.—el hermano,   *the brother.*   los hermanos,   *the brothers.*
   la silla,   *the chair.*   las sillas,   *the chairs.*

(*b*) with an accented **e**.

Ex.—el pie,   *the foot.*   los pies,   *the feet.*
   el café,   *the coffee (coffee-house).*   los cafés,   *the coffees.*

(2) By adding **es** to the singular when the noun ends:

(*a*) with a consonant.

Ex.—la flor,   *the flower.*   las flores,   *the flowers.*
   el mes,   *the month.*   los meses,   *the months.*

(*b*) with **y**.

Ex.—el rey,   *the king.*   los reyes,   *the kings.*
   la ley,   *the law.*   las leyes,   *the laws.*

(*c*) with an accented vowel (except **e**).

Ex.—el rubí,   *the ruby.*   los rubíes,   *the rubies.*

(Except **papá**, **mamá**, which give **papás**, **mamás** in the plural.)

REMARK.—Final **z** is changed to **c** before **es** (see § **6**).

Ex.—el juez,   *the judge.*   los jueces,   *the judges.*
   la voz,   *the voice.*   las voces,   *the voices.*

28. Nouns ending in **s** do not change in the plural when the last syllable is unaccented, otherwise they follow the general rule and add **es**.

Ex.—el lunes,   *Monday.*   los lunes,   *Mondays.*
   la crisis,   *the crisis.*   las crisis,   *the crises.*
but: el Inglés,   *the Englishman.*   los Ingleses,   *the Englishmen.*

29. Compound nouns ending in **s** do not change in the

plural. Other compound nouns follow the rule given for single nouns.

Ex.—el cortaplumas, *the penknife.* los cortaplumas, *the knives.*
la vanagloria, *vainglory.* las vanaglorias, *the vainglories.*
el ferrocarril, *the railroad.* los ferrocarriles, *the railroads.*

(Except **gentilhombre,** *nobleman,* which gives **gentileshombres.**)

EXERCISE II.

VOCABULARY II.

(Words given in the preceding Chapter, and in the first part of the exercise.)

I. Put the definite article before the following words; write also the plural form of both article and nouns, as: **el hombre, los hombres.**

Hombre, *man;* mujer, *woman;* rey, *king;* juez, *judge;* reina, *queen;* albañil, *mason;* gallina, *hen;* marinero, *sailor;* dinero, *money;* silla, *chair;* mesa, *table;* libertad, *liberty;* virtud, *virtue;* río, *river;* martes, *Tuesday;* ojo, *eye;* calle, *street;* árbol, *tree;* mano, *hand;* día, *day.*

A. 1. El rey tiene un palacio y el juez tiene una casa. 2. Tengo flores muy bonitas. 3. El Rín es un río. 4. Mi padre da un cortaplumas á mi hermano. 5. La Habana y Santiago son ciudades de Cuba.

B. 1. The Englishman is the brother of the judge. 2. The railroad gives life [1] to the city. 3. The sailor has money. 4. The mason's [2] sister is a [3] seamstress. 5. The king's palace. 6. The tree has flowers. 7. The cities of the nation. 8. The queen's jewels.

---

[1] animación.　[2] see § **18.**　[3] see § **17.**

CHAPTER III.

FORMATION OF THE FEMININE IN NOUNS.—AUGMENTATIVES AND DIMINUTIVES

30. The feminine of nouns representing living beings, can often be formed from the masculine by a slight change in the termination.

(1) Nouns ending in **o** change **o** to **a**:

Ex.—el hermano, *the brother.*   la hermana, *the sister.*
  el tío,   *the uncle.*   la tía,   *the aunt.*
  un gato,   *a cat* (male).   una gata,   *a cat* (female).

(2) Nouns ending in **l, n, r, s**, add **a**.

Ex.—el Español, *the Spaniard.*   la Española, *the Spanish woman.*
  el león,   *the lion.*   la leona,   *the lioness.*
  el señor,   *the gentleman.*   la señora,   *the lady.*
  el marqués, *the marquis.*   la marquesa, *the marchioness.*

31. The following are more irregular in the formation of the feminine:

conde,   *count,*   condesa.   rey,   *king,*   reina.
duque,   *duke,*   duquesa.   príncipe, *prince,* princesa.
barón,   *baron,*   baronesa.   actor,   *actor,*   actriz.
Don,   *Mr.*   Doña.

NOTE.—*Don* and *Doña* are used only before Christian names, *Señor* and *Señora* before family names.

Ex.—Don José Herrera,   *Mr. Joseph Herrera.*
  Señor Herrera,   *Mr. Herrera* (el señor Herrera, *when not addressed*).

32. The plural form of certain masculine nouns, indicating relationship and titles, is sometimes used to designate both the masculine and the feminine.

Ex.—los padres,   *the fathers,*   or   *the father and mother.*
los hermanos,   *the brothers,*   or   *the brother and sister.*
los reyes,   *the kings,*   or   *the king and queen.*
los príncipes,   *the princes,*   or   *the prince and princess.*

AUGMENTATIVES AND DIMINUTIVES

33. The Spanish language is peculiarly rich in suffixes which are added to nouns, adjectives, and adverbs, to modify their ordinary meaning. These suffixes are called: (*a*) augmentative, when they indicate increase in size or quality; (*b*) diminutive, when they indicate importance or size less than normal. In addition to the idea of greater or lesser size, these suffixes often imply coarseness, ugliness, irony, or attractiveness, nicety and affection. To use them properly, much familiarity with the language is necessary.

But as they are often met with, especially in familiar style, the most common of these suffixes are given here.

1. Augmentatives

34. –on, –ote, –azo, and their feminine forms, –ona, –ota, –aza, denote greater size or quality, with or without an idea of grotesqueness, ugliness, etc.

Ex.—silla,   *chair.*   sillón,   *big chair, easy chair.*
mujer,   *woman.*   mujerona,   *big woman.*
discurso,   *speech.*   discursote,   *long, tiresome speech.*
feo,   *ugly.*   feote,   *very ugly.*
libro,   *book.*   librazo,   *big book.*
boca,   *mouth.*   bocaza,   *large mouth.*

Note.—The endings **azo, ada,** often indicate a blow or

injury due to the thing named by the noun to which they
are added.

Ex.—fusil,   *gun.*   fusilazo,   *gun-shot.*
    cuchillo,   *knife.*   cuchillada,   *knife-thrust, knife-wound.*

2. Diminutives

35. The most common of these suffixes are : –ito (–cito,
–ecito), –illo, –uelo, –ete, with their feminine forms, –ita
(–cita, –ecita), –illa, –uela, –eta.   They convey the idea of
smallness, nicety, attractiveness, affection, etc.   The endings
–illo, –uelo, often have a depreciative meaning.

Ex.—hermano,   *brother.*   hermanito,   *little brother.*
    casa,   *house.*   casita,   *nice, little house.*
    mano, (*fem.*)   *hand.*   manecita,   *pretty, little hand.*
    autor,   *author.*   autorcillo,   *poor author.*
    plaza,   *square.*   plazuela,   *little, ill-kept square.*

36. It will be noticed that augmentatives and diminutives
are added to the full form of words ending in a consonant
or accented vowel, and that words ending in an unaccented
vowel, lose that vowel before adding the termination.

EXERCISE III.

VOCABULARY III.

es,*   *is.* ⎱ inherent   está,*   *is.* ⎱ accidental
son,   *are.* ⎰ or permanent.   están,   *are.* ⎰ or temporary.
    quiero,   *I want.*   tienen,   *have.*   en,   *in.*
    quiere,   *wants.*   muchacho,   *boy.*

(Also words given in preceding Chapter.)

* See § **151.**

A. 1. El perro y el gato son animales útiles. 2. El señor conde de X... es mi tío; la señora condesa es hermana de mi madre. 3. Mi hermanito quiere un cuchillo y un fusil. 4. Los reyes y los príncipes están en el palacio del duque. 5. Don José Herrera es español y la señora Herrera es inglesa. 6. El autorcillo tiene un librazo. 7. Mis padres (*or* mi padre y mi madre) están en Madrid. 8. La manecita de la marquesa. 9. El marinero quiere dinero. 10. Quiero libros, plumas y papel.

B. 1. My father is in Madrid; he[1] is a merchant and has a house in Alcalá street[2]. 2. The countess gives a hat to my little sister. 3. She[1] has flowers in her[7] little hand. 4. Madrid and Toledo are cities of Spain.[3] 5. I want paper and ink, and my brother wants a small book.[4] 6. The boy gives a flower to the little girl.[4] 7. The king and the queen have a palace in Seville.[5] 8. The captain gives money to the sailor. 9. The city of Havana has streets and palaces, lanes[6] and ill-kept squares.

[1] omit.   [2] transl.: in the street of A.   [3] España.   [4] transl. in one word.
[5] Sevilla.   [6] callejuelas.   [7] su.

CHAPTER IV.

ADJECTIVES

37. Adjectives agree in gender and number with the noun they qualify. An adjective qualifying two singular nouns, is usually masculine plural (unless both nouns are feminine when the adjective is feminine plural).

Ex.—Un libro nuevo,   *A new book.*
Una casa nueva,   *A new house.*
El padre y la madre   *The father and mother*
son buenos,   *are good.*

Formation of the Feminine

38. Most adjectives end in **o** in the masculine, and change **o** to **a** to form the feminine.

Ex.—Un hombre rico.   *A rich man.*
Una mujer rica.   *A rich woman.*

39. Barring a few exceptions, adjectives ending in a consonant, or a vowel other than **o**, do not change in the feminine.

Ex.—Un hombre prudente, capaz   *A man prudent, capable*
y fiel.   *and faithful.*
Una mujer prudente, capaz y fiel.   *A woman,* etc.

40. Exceptions :

(1) Adjectives indicating nationality, and ending in a consonant, add **a** to form the feminine.

Ex.—español, española,   *Spanish.*   but : suizo, suiza,   *Swiss.*
francés, francesa,   *French.*

(2) A few adjectives ending in **an** and **on** add **a** in the feminine.

Ex.—holgazán, holgazana, *lazy.* burlón, burlona, *roguish.*

(3) Those ending in **or**, not having a comparative value, add **a** in the feminine.

Ex.—protector, protectora,   *protecting.*
     traidor, traidora,   *treacherous.*
but: inferior (*masc.*), inferior (*fem.*),   *inferior.*

Formation of the Plural

41. Adjectives form their plural, in both genders, in the same manner as nouns of similar endings.

EXERCISE IV.

VOCABULARY IV.

el amigo,	*the friend (masc.)*	la amiga,	*the friend (fem.)*
el vecino,	*the neighbor.*	la vecina,	*the neighbor.*
el hijo,	*the son.*	la hija,	*the daughter.*
hermoso, bello,	*beautiful.*	feliz,	*happy.*
pequeño,	*small.*	infeliz,	*unhappy.*
grande,	*large.*	ancho,	*wide, broad.*
blanco,	*white.*	negro,	*black.*
muy,	*very.*	malo,	*bad.*

pero,   *but.*

(Also words given in preceding Chapter.)

A. 1. El hijo del comerciante es un muchacho prudente y capaz. 2. Mi vecino es rico pero infeliz. 3. Las casas blancas de la calle de Málaga son muy hermosas. 4. Una mala pluma es una amiga traidora. 5. La reina tiene alhajas muy hermosas.   6. El perro es un animal fiel y útil.   7. El muchacho quiere tinta negra y papel blanco.   8. Los padres de mi amigo son españoles.

B. 1. The Amazon[1] is a very[2] large[2] river.   2. The merchant is very rich; he[3] has houses in the city and estates in the country.[4]   3. My friend's son is a very[2] lazy[2] boy.   4. The French nation has good laws.   5. The boys and girls have roguish[2] eyes.   6. Paris is a beautiful city; it[3] has broad streets and large squares.✕ 7. The houses of Cadiz are very white.   8. My sister and the judge's daughter are good friends.

[1] El Amazonas.   [2] follow the noun; for position of adj., see § **44, 47, 51.**   [3] omit.   [4] el campo.

CHAPTER V.

APOCOPATION

42. The following adjectives lose their final **o** when they immediately precede a noun in the masculine singular.

bueno,	*good.*	ninguno,	*none, not any.*
malo,	*bad.*	primero,	*first.*
uno,	*one.*	tercero,	*third.*
alguno,	*some, any.*	postrero,	*last.*

Bueno and **malo** must immediately precede the noun which they modify, the others admit the insertion of an adjective.

Ex.—el buen vecino,	*the good neighbor.*
mal tiempo,	*bad weather.*
un poeta,	*a poet.*
un célebre poeta,	*a celebrated poet.*
algún día,	*some day.*
ningún hombre,	*no man.*
el primer capítulo,	*the first chapter.*

In other cases the full form of the adjective is used.

Ex.—el hombre bueno,	*the good man.*
vino malo,	*bad wine.*
el libro tercero,	*the third book.*
el primero de julio,	*the first of July.*

43. Grande, usually becomes **gran** before a noun of either gender beginning with a consonant (except **h**), especially when used to indicate eminence.

> Ex.—un gran general,   *a great general.*
> una gran casa,   *a great family.*

NOTE.—In emphatic expressions the full form is used in all cases.

> Ex.—un grande sacrificio,   *a great sacrifice.*

44. When **grande** refers to size, it regularly stands after the noun.

> Ex.—un palacio grande,   *a large palace.*
> una casa grande,   *a large house.*

45. Santo, *Saint*, becomes **San** before names of Saints or Holy men.

> Ex.—San Pablo,   *St. Paul.*   San Juan,   *St. John.*

excepting : **Santo Tomás**, *St. Thomas,** **Santo Domingo**, *St. Dominick.*

46. Ciento, *hundred*, becomes **cien** before a word which it multiplies, allowing, however, the insertion of an adjective.

> Ex.—cien hombres,   *one hundred men.*
> cien valerosos soldados,   *one hundred brave soldiers.*
> cien mil pesos,   *one hundred thousand dollars.*
> but : ciento y diez hombres,   *one hundred and ten men.*
> mil y ciento,   *one thousand one hundred.*

POSITION OF THE ADJECTIVE

47. The adjective, in Spanish, generally follows the noun, but most writers place it according to their idea of effect and harmony. The tendency of the language being to make the more important word follow the less important, an adjective will come before the noun when the latter is the

---

* The island of St. Thomas in the West Indies is called in Spanish : San Tŏmas.

principal word, and after when the adjective assumes the chief importance.

48. From the above, it follows that an adjective denoting a quality belonging to the noun as a matter of course will precede.

| Ex.—la dulce miel, | *the sweet honey.* |
| la blanca nieve, | *the white snow.* |

When expressing an occasional quality, the adjective follows.

| Ex.—el agua fría, | *the cold water.* |
| el vino blanco, | *the white wine.* |

(Water is not always cold; wine, not always white.)

49. Generally, a long adjective will follow a short noun, and a long noun will follow a short adjective, especially when there is quite a difference in the number of syllables, unless a different order is needed for emphasis.

| Ex.—una cosa imposible, | *an impossible thing.* |
| la ancha galería, | *the wide gallery.* |

50. Some adjectives have a different meaning according to whether they precede or follow the noun.

Ex.—pobre hombre,	*unfortunate man.*
hombre pobre,	*indigent man.*
una buena noche,	*a good night.**
Noche Buena,	*Christmas eve.*

51. As it has been stated in § **33**, the common meaning of an adjective may be altered by the addition of augmentative or diminutive suffixes.

| Ex.—rico, | *rich.* | ricote, | *very rich (depreciative).* |
| nuevo, | *new.* | nuevecito, | *" brand new."* |

NOTE.—Augmentatives and diminutives follow their noun.

* As a salutation, Good night is *Buenas noches;* Good day is *Buenos días;* Good afternoon is *Buenas tardes.*

EXERCISE V.

VOCABULARY V.

No, *not** (placed before the verb).

(Also words given in preceding Chapter.)

A. 1. Los soldados son valerosos, pero no tienen un buen general.   2. El postrer día del mes; el primer capítulo del libro.   3. Quiero ir (*to go*) á San Juan de Puerto Rico, pero no tengo dinero.   4. El pobre hombre tiene las simpatías (*sympathies*) de sus (*his*) vecinos.   5. La casa de mi amigo es una hermosa casa blanca.   6. Un buen hombre siempre (*always*) tiene buenos amigos.   7. Cien soldados y un capitán están en la plaza.   8. El hombre pobre no tiene dinero, pero es feliz.

B. 1. The first day and the first night of the month. 2. The boy has paper and ink; he[1] wants a good pen. 3. My father gives a glass[2] of white wine to the sailor. 4. The prince wants the King's crown.[3]   5. The third chapter of the new book.   6. Tuesday is the first day of July. 7. The boy wants the soldier's gun.   8. My neighbor is a happy man; he[1] has good sons-and-daughters[4], and faithful friends.   9. The soldiers do[1] not want to go[5] to the King's palace.   10. A prudent father gives good books to his children.[6]

---

* The English *do, does*, is omitted in Spanish.

[1] omit.   [2] una copa.   [3] la corona.   [4] express in one word.   [5] see A.3; [6] same as note 4.

CHAPTER VI.

COMPARISON

52. Spanish adjectives, barring a few exceptions, form their different degrees of comparison by means of adverbs, and not by a change in the termination.

COMPARATIVE

53. The comparative is obtained by placing **más**, *more*, or **menos**, *less*, before the adjective.

Ex.—rico,   *rich.*   más rico,   *richer.*
     triste,   *sad.*   menos triste, *less sad.*

54. Besides the regularly formed comparative, four adjectives have another comparative, derived from the Latin, which is more commonly used. They are:

bueno,   *good.*   mejor, *better,*   rarely más bueno.
malo,   *bad, poor.*   peor, *worse,*   "   más malo.
grande, *large.*   mayor, *larger (older),** or más grande.
pequeño, *small, little.* menor, *smaller (younger),** or más pequeño.

55. The word *than* which in English precedes the second member of the comparison, is rendered in Spanish as follows:

(1) By **que** in ordinary comparison when both members are of the same nature.

Ex.—la nieve es más fría que el   *The snow is colder than the*
     agua,   *water.*

---

* *Mayor* and *menor* when applied to persons usually signify *older* and *younger.*

(2) By **de** when it precedes a numerical expression in an affirmative sentence; otherwise **que** is preferred.

Ex.—tengo más de diez libros,   *I have more than ten books.*
but : no tengo más que dos,   *I haven't more than two.*

(3) By **de lo que** when the second term of the comparison contains a verb, which could be followed in English by a repetition of the verb used in the first term.

Ex.—Es más rico de lo que dice.   *He is richer than he says (he is).*

SUPERLATIVE

56. The superlative is either relative or absolute. It is relative when expressing the highest (or lowest) degree of any quality in comparison with others expressed or implied. It is absolute when there is no comparison.

Relative Superlative

57. The relative superlative is obtained by placing the definite article, or a possessive adjective, before the comparative.

Ex.—blanco,   *white.*   más blanco,   *whiter.*
     el más blanco, *the whitest.*   mi mejor amigo, *my best friend.*

58. The position of the superlative is the same as that of the positive adjective, but when placed after the noun the article is not repeated.

Ex.—la más hermosa calle }
   or la calle más hermosa, } *the most beautiful street.*
     el clima más frío,   *the coldest climate.*

59. The prepositions *of, in*, which in English follow a superlative, are rendered into Spanish by **de**, sometimes **entre**, *among*.

Ex.—el hombre más virtuoso   *the most virtuous man*
        de la ciudad.   *in town.*
     el médico más sabio del   *the wisest doctor in the*
        país.   *country.*

Absolute Superlative

60. The absolute superlative is formed :

(1) By means of adverbs placed before the adjective, such as **muy**, *very*, **sumamente**, *extremely*, **excesivamente**, *exceedingly*, etc.

Ex.—muy útil,   *very useful.*
  sumamente prudente, *extremely prudent.*

(2) By adding the augmentative termination **–ísimo**, which is inflected like an adjective in **o**.

Ex.—utilísimo, *very useful.* prudentísimo, *very prudent.*

61. The termination **–ísimo** is added directly to a consonant ending, or takes the place of a final vowel (or diphthong).

Ex.—hábil, habilísimo, *very skillful.*
  simple, simplísimo, *very simple.*
  soberbio, soberbísimo, *very fine (superb).*
  limpio, limpísimo, *very clean.*
but: impío, impiísimo, *very wicked.*
  frío, friísimo, *very cold.*

(*a*) **c**, **g** and **z** become respectively **qu**, **gu** and **c** before **–ísimo**. (See §6.)

Ex.—rico, riquísimo, *very rich.* vago, vaguísimo, *very vague.*
    capaz, capacísimo, *very capable.*

(*b*) The tonic diphthongs **ie** and **ue**, return usually to their original vowels **e** and **o** when they lose the tonic accent.

Ex.—bueno, bonísimo, *very* fuerte, fortísimo, *very strong.*
  good.   cierto, certísimo, *very sure.*

(*c*) The ending **ble** becomes **bil**, and a few adjectives in **–ro**, **–re**, change that syllable to **érrimo** *

Ex.—noble, nobilísimo, *very* libre, libérrimo, *very free.*
  noble.   mísero, misérrimo, *very wretched.*

* *Cf.* Latin : *errimus.*

(*d*) Several adjectives revert to the original Latin form before adding –ísimo.

Ex.—fiel,   *faithful.*   fidelísimo,   *very faithful.*
    sabio,   *wise.*   sapientísimo,   *very wise.*

62. The superlative in –ísimo means more than the one obtained by the addition of **muy**; thus: **una ciudad hermosísima**, is a stronger expression than **una ciudad muy hermosa**.

Comparative of Equality

63. The comparison of equality is expressed by means of **tan, como**, or simply **como**.

Ex.—tan rico como su padre,   *as rich as his father.*
    duro como una piedra,   *as hard as a stone.*

64. Before a noun, the adjective **tant–o** (–a, –os, –as) is used instead of the adverb **tan**.

Ex.—tanto oro como plata,   *as much gold as silver.*
    tanta prudencia como
       valor,   *as much prudence as valor.*

EXERCISE VI.

VOCABULARY VI.

(Words given in preceding Chapter.)

A. 1. La casa del conde es más grande que el palacio del rey.   2. Mi vecino es un hombre rico; tiene más dinero de lo que dice.   3. De las dos hermanas, la mayor (§54, *note*) es la más prudente, la menor, la más hermosa.   4. El hijo del comerciante es menos hábil que su amigo.   5. La calle de Alcalá es la más hermosa de Madrid.   6. Mi mejor amigo está en París.   7. Un perro es un amigo muy fiel (*or* fidelísimo).   8. No tengo más que dos caballos (*horses*), pero mi amigo tiene más de diez.

B. 1. Paris is larger than New York; it[1] has broader streets and more beautiful squares. 2. The houses of Cadiz are as white as snow; but the streets are not always[2] clean. 3. The merchant has more money than the sailor; he[1] is the richest man in the city. 4. Iron[3] is very useful[6]; it[1] is more useful than gold[4] and silver.[5] 5. The judge has not so many houses as the merchant. 6. He[1] is a very wise[6] man. 7. The climate of New York is not very cold. 8. The mechanic[7] has less money than the merchant but he[1] is happier.

[1] Omit. [2] siempre. [3] hierro (*masc.*, *cf.* **13**, a.) [4] (*masc.*) [5] (*fem.*)
[6] Express in two ways. [7] artesano.

CHAPTER VII.

NUMERALS

Cardinals

65. The cardinal numerals are:

0 cero	10 diez	20 veinte
1 un–o, –a.	11 once	21 veinte y uno *
2 dos	12 doce	22 veinte y dos, etc.
3 tres	13 trece	30 treinta
4 cuatro	14 catorce	40 cuarenta
5 cinco	15 quince	50 cincuenta
6 seis	16 diez y seis *	60 sesenta
7 siete	17 diez y siete	70 setenta
8 ocho	18 diez y ocho	80 ochenta
9 nueve	19 diez y nueve	90 noventa

100 ciento	200 doscientos	300 trescientos
500 quinientos	700 setecientos	900 novecientos

(Others regularly formed.)

1,000 mil   2,000 dos mil, etc.   100,000 cien mil

200,000 doscient–os (–as) mil, etc.

1,000,000 un millón, or un cuento.

66. All cardinal numbers are invariable, except **uno** and the compounds of **ciento**.

Ex.—cinco casas,   *five houses.*

veinte y cuatro personas, *twenty-four persons.*

67. Uno is treated like an ordinary adjective, and agrees with the noun. It loses the **o** before a masculine noun. (See § **42.**)

Ex.—un libro, *a book, one book.*   una casa, *one house, a house.*

---

* The compounds *diez y seis, diez y siete . . . veinte y uno, veinte y dos,* etc. . . . are sometimes written in one word: *dieciséis, diecisiete . . . veintiuno, veintidos,* etc.

68. For apocopation of **ciento**, see § **46**.

69. Compounds of **ciento** are treated like regular adjectives.

Ex.—doscientos pasos,	*two hundred steps.*
setecientas personas,	*seven hundred persons.*
cuatrocientas mil almas,	*four hundred thousand souls.*

70. Tens of hundreds must always be expressed by **mil.**

Ex.—1899, mil ochocientos noventa y nueve.

(**Y,** *and,* is used only before the last number.)

71. The cardinals are used instead of the ordinals :

(*a*) In speaking of the days of the month, except the first which is **primero.**

Ex.—el diez y siete de abril,	*April 17th.*
el primero de enero,	*January 1st.*

(*b*) With names of sovereigns from and including eleventh, upwards.

Ex.—Alfonso trece,	*Alphonso the Thirteenth.*
Luis once, Luis catorce,	*Louis the Eleventh, Louis the Fourteenth.*
but: Carlos Quinto,	*Charles the Fifth.*

(*c*) In ordinary language, when speaking of chapters, pages, etc.

Ex.—libro quince,	*fifteenth book.*
el siglo diez y nueve,	*the nineteenth century.*
página treinta y dos,	*page thirty-two.*

Ordinals

72. The ordinal numerals are :

1st	primero	5th	quinto
2d	segundo	6th	sexto (or sesto)
3d	tercero	7th	séptimo (or sétimo)
4th	cuarto	8th	octavo

9th	noveno (or nono)		70th	septuagésimo
10th	décimo		80th	octogésimo
11th	undécimo		90th	nonagésimo
12th	duodécimo		100th	centésimo
13th	décimo tercio		101st	centésimo primo
14th	décimo cuarto		200th	ducentésimo
15th	décimo quinto, etc.		300th	trecentésimo
20th	vigésimo		400th	cuadragentésimo
21st	vigésimo primo, etc.		500th	quingentésimo
30th	trigésimo		600th	sexcentésimo
31st	trigésimo primo, etc.		700th	septengentésimo
40th	cuadragésimo		800th	octogentésimo
50th	quincuagésimo		900th	nonagentésimo
60th	sexagésimo		1,000th	milésimo
		1,000,000th	millonésimo	

73. All ordinal numbers are treated like adjectives, and agree in gender and number with their noun.

Ex.—las primeras páginas,   *the first pages.*
     escena décima cuarta,   *fourteenth scene.*

74. For apocopation of **primero** and **tercero**, see § **42**.

EXERCISE VII.

VOCABULARY VII.

el año,	*the year.*	la mitad,	*the half (noun).*
el minuto,	*the minute.*	medi–o (–a),	*half (adj.)*
la hora,	*the hour.*	Qué,	*What.*
hay,	*there is, there are.*	¿Qué hora es?*	*What time is it?*
	los Estados Unidos,	*the United States.*	

(Also words given in preceding Chapter.)

A. 1. El mes de enero tiene treinta y un días, y un día tiene veinte y cuatro horas. 2. ¿Qué hora es? Es la una;

---

* Interrogative (or exclamative) sentences require an inverted interrogation (or exclamation) point before the sentence. See § **233**.

son las cinco y media; son las siete y cuarto; son las diez menos cuarto; son las dos y diez minutos; son las ocho menos veinte. 3. En la ciudad de la Habana hay más de cien mil almas. 4. Los Estados Unidos tienen más de setenta millones de habitantes. 5. El muchacho quiere seis naranjas y nueve manzanas (*apples*). 6. Hay quinientas páginas en mi libro. 7. El buen muchacho da la mitad de su manzana á su hermanita. 8. La escena tercera es mejor que la primera.

B. Three and six are[1] nine and five are[1] fourteen and twelve are[1] twenty-six. 2. April is the fourth month of the year, and July, the seventh. 3. The fourth of July is a great holiday[2] in the United States. 4. In time[3] of peace, Spain has more than 75,000 soldiers, and France more than 500,000. 5. A year has 12 months and 365 days. 6. What time is it? It is twenty minutes past nine; it is a quarter to one; it is half past three. 7. He gives half of his money to the poor.[4] 8. The year 1492 is in the second half of the fifteenth century.

[1] Omitted in calculation.   [2] día festivo.   [3] tiempo.   [4] (*plural*).

CHAPTER VIII.

PERSONAL PRONOUNS

Subject Pronouns

75. Personal pronouns used as the subjects of verbs are generally omitted, unless needed for emphasis, or to avoid ambiguity when the verb form would not by its ending indicate clearly the person and number of the subject.

76. The subject pronouns are:

		Singular		Plural	
1st pers.		yo,	*I.*	nosotr–os (–as),	*we.*
2d pers.	{	tú,	*thou.*		
		vos,	*you.*	vosotr–os (–as),	*you.*
3d pers.	*masc.*	él,	*he.*	ellos,	*they (masc.)*
	fem.	ella,	*she.*	ellas,	*they (fem.)*
	neuter.	ello,	*(it).*		
	Usted,	*You (masc. and fem.)*		Ustedes,	*You (masc. and fem.)*

77. Tú, *thou* (to be translated generally by *you*), is more commonly used in Spanish than in English. It is employed: in sacred or poetical style; between intimate friends and near relatives; in addressing children, servants, animals.

Vos, *you,* although limited to one person, requires the verb in the second person plural. It is used: interchangeably with **tú,** in sacred style; in representing ancient manners; by children to elders; as a mark of scorn or anger to inferiors; in translation to represent the "you" and "vous" of English and French.

78. Usted (*plur.* **ustedes**), usually written **V.** or **Vd.** (*plur.* **V.V.** or **Vds.**), is a contraction of the now obsolete: **Vuestra**

34

merced, *your grace* (*plur.* **vuestras mercedes**). This form, which represents the conventional English " you," is the universal address of society and the only one a foreigner is likely to use. It is treated as a noun, and requires the verb, object pronouns, and possessives in the third person singular or plural.

Ex.—Usted tiene,   *You have,* literally : *your grace has.*

(*Cf.* the English usage in addressing a judge : *Your Honor has . . .*)

79. When expressed, the subject pronouns may either precede or follow the verb, according to the writers idea of elegance, harmony, etc.

Ex.—Yo volveré pronto, ⎫
      Volveré yo pronto, ⎬   *I shall return soon.*
                 ⎭

Object Pronouns

80. Personal object pronouns can be divided into *conjunctive* and *disjunctive* or *prepositional.* The conjunctive forms are those used as the direct object of a verb, or as the indirect object without a preposition. The disjunctive forms are those used independently of a verb, or as the object of a preposition.

The personal object pronouns are :

Conjunctive		Disjunctive	
me,	*me, to me.*	mí,	*me.*
te,	*thee, to thee.*	tí,	*thee.*
le (lo *),	*him,* ⎰ *to him.*	él,	*him.*
la,	*her,* le, ⎱		
lo,	*it.* ⎰ *to her.*	ella,	*her.*

* See foot note on page 36.

Conjunctive		Disjunctive	
nos,	*us, to us.*	nosotr–os (–as),	*us.*
os,	*you, to you.*	vosotr–os (–as),	*you.*
los (les *),	*them (masc.)*	ellos,	*them (m.)*
las,	*them (fem.)*	ellas,	*them (f.)*
les,	*to them (masc. and fem.)*		
se,	*reflexive 3d. pers., masc. and fem., s. and pl.*	sí,	*reflexive masc. and fem., s. and pl.*

81. The conjunctive object pronoun regularly precedes the verb; in compound tenses, the auxiliaries.

Ex.—Me llama,   *He calls me.*
  Te digo,   *I tell thee.*
  Le hablan,   *They speak to him (to her).*

82. With infinitives, present participles, and affirmative imperatives, the pronoun is joined to the verb, forming a single word.

Ex.—llamándome, *calling me.*
  decirte,   *to tell thee.*
  díle,   *tell (2d sing.) him (her).*

NOTE.—The pronoun is also joined to any verb tense in the affirmative when it is the first word of a sentence: **Pláceme, dijo el juez,** . . . *It pleases me, said the judge,* . . .

83. The final **s** and **d** of the 1st and 2d persons plural of the imperative are omitted when **nos** and **os** are appended.

Ex.—Defendámonos *for* Defendámosnos, *Let us defend ourselves.*
  Defendéos *for* Defendedos,   *Defend yourselves.*

Exception: **idos,** *go (ye).*

84. When an infinitive is governed by another verb, the

---

* The form *lo* is often employed instead of *le* as the masculine accusative when speaking of inanimate objects, *le* being used for persons, animals, or personified things. In the same way *les* is sometimes used for *los; les* referring to persons, *los* to things.

pronoun is usually added to the infinitive, but it may also precede the first verb.

Ex.—Voy á verle,
or : Le voy á ver, } *I am going to see him.*

NOTE.—A pronoun should not be appended to the infinitive of a verb which does not admit of an object, ex.: **le permito dormir,** *I allow him to sleep ;* **permito dormirle** would be inadmissible.

85. When two conjunctive object pronouns are governed by one verb, they are both placed before or after as a single pronoun should be. The dative precedes the accusative, but the reflexive **se** always stands first, no matter what its case may be. Two such pronouns cannot be separated by any other word.

Ex.—Me lo dice,   *He says it to me.*
Nos los promete,   *He promises them to us.*
sin decírmelo,   *without telling it to me.*
Démelo,   *Give it to me.*

86. If both object pronouns are in the third person, the dative, singular or plural, takes the form **se** to avoid the repetition of the l.

Ex.—Se lo da, *for* Le lo da,   *He gives it to him (her).*
Se los mando, " Les los mando, *I send them to them.*

87. As this construction would often cause ambiguity, a disjunctive pronoun corresponding to the one replaced by **se** may be added to the verb.

Ex.—Se lo da á él,   *He gives it to him.*
Se lo da á ella,   *He gives it to her.*

(*Cf.* redundant construction § 92.)

NOTE.—When two object pronouns are used with a verb, both are placed before the verb only when the accusative is the pronoun of the third person. If the accusative is a pronoun of the first or second person, the dative is placed after the verb, and assumes the disjunctive form.

Ex.—Me la envia,	*He sends her to me.*
Me envia á ella,	*He sends me to her.*
Me envia á tí,	*He sends me to thee.*

88. As stated above, in § **78**, **usted** is treated as a noun, and can only be replaced by an appropriate conjunctive pronoun of the third person.

Ex.—Busqué á V. pero no le encontré.	*I looked for you but I did not find you.*
Me ha engañado V., señora, pero yo la perdono.	*You have deceived me, madam, but I forgive you.*

89. As every noun in Spanish is either masculine or feminine, the neuter pronoun **lo** cannot refer to a definite noun, but it is used to represent a phrase, a quality, or an idea to which no gender can be assigned.

Ex.—No lo creo,	*I do not believe it (i.e. What is said.)*
¿Está V. enfermo? Lo soy.	*Are you sick? I am.*

NOTE.—Confusion between the neuter **lo**, and **lo** used instead of **le** must be avoided.

90. When the pronoun is the object of a preposition, the disjunctive form is required. It does not necessarily stand next to the verb.

Ex.—Trae una carta para mí,	*He brings a letter for me.*
Hablamos de él,	*We speak of him.*

91. The preposition **con**, *with*, is joined to **mí, tí, sí**, and **go**

s added, giving the forms: **conmigo**, *with me*, **contigo**, *with thee*, **consigo**, *with himself* (*herself, themselves, masc. and fem., yourself, yourselves*).

92. The disjunctive form of the pronoun is often used with the conjunctive form, for the purpose of clearness or emphasis. It may follow the verb or precede the conjunctive, the latter form giving greater emphasis. This is called the redundant construction.

Ex.—Me gusta,
Me gusta á mí (*emphatic*),
Á mí me gusta (*more emphatic*), } *It pleases me.*

Se lo digo,   *I say it to him.*
Se lo digo á él (*or* : á   *I say it to him* (*or* : *to her,*
ella, á ellos, á ellas),   *to them, masc. and fem.*)

EXERCISE VIII.

VOCABULARY VIII.

V. tiene,   *You have.*   ¿Tiene V.*?   *Have you?*

ó,   *or.*

(Also words and verb forms given in preceding Chapter.)

A. 1. ¿Tiene V. las llaves de la casa? No las tengo pero mi hermano las tiene. 2. Mis amigos están en la ciudad; voy á verlos; quiero decirles que mi padre está enfermo. 3. Nos llama el hijo del vecino; trae una carta para mí, y otra para tí (*or* V.) 4. No quiero ir (*to go*) con V.V. á la casa del juez. 5. Mi amigo quiere naranjas; tengo dos ó

* In questions, subject usually follows the verb, but note that subject may also follow in positive sentences. *Cf.* § **79** and *A.* 3.

tres y se las mando. 6. Á mí me dice Juan (*John*) que su tío tiene más de cien mil pesos, pero yo no lo creo. 7. ¿ Me da V. el libro á mí ó á mi hermano? 8. Pedro (*Peter*) no quiere ir al teatro (*theater*) conmigo.

B. The boy wants oranges, and his father gives them to him. 2. We speak of her uncle and of her. 3. I tell you[1]; I tell it to you[1]. 4. He has a book; he gives it to you[1] (to me, to us, to her). 5. Have you a letter for me or for him? 6. The theater[2] does not please me[1]; it[3] does not please him[1]. 7. I have a letter for the merchant, and I am going to send it to him. 8. They speak of her, of you, and of me.

[1] Give ordinary and emphatic forms. [2] See A. 8. [3] Omit.

CHAPTER IX.

POSSESSIVES

93. The possessive adjectives and pronouns agree in gender and number with the object possessed, and *not* with the possessor.

Ex.—el padre y la hija suya,   *the father and his daughter.*
   el libro mío,   *my book.*
   la casa nuestra,   *our house.*

Possessive Adjectives

94. These adjectives are :

mío,	*my.*	nuestro,	*our.*
tuyo,	*thy.*	vuestro,	*your.*
suyo,	*his, her, your.*	suyo,	*their, your.*

The above are inflected like any adjective ending in **o**. They regularly stand after the noun which is usually accompanied by the definite article.

Ex.—el hermano mío,   *my brother.*
   la prima suya,   *his (her, their, your) cousin (fem.)*
        See § 96-97.
   las sillas vuestras,   *your chairs.*
   los caballos tuyos,   *thy horses.*

95. The preceding construction is preferred when emphasis is required; in ordinary language, however, the adjectives precede the noun, and **mío, tuyo, suyo,** become **mi, tu, su,** for both genders, adding **s** in the plural.

Ex.—mi hermano,   *my brother.*
   su pluma,   *his (her, their or your) pen.* See § 96.

nuestro libro,	*our book.*
vuestras sillas,	*your chairs.*
tus caballos,	*thy horses.*

96. As the adjective **su** does not indicate clearly the possessor, and means *his, her, its, their, your*, it is often necessary to add to the noun a personal pronoun preceded by **de**.

Ex.—su sombrero de él (*or :*   *his (or her) hat.*
     de ella),
  sus casas de ellas,   *their (fem.) houses.*

also in omitting **su**: **las casas de ellas.**

97. As *you* is generally rendered by **Usted** (*3d pers.*), the possessive *your* is expressed by **su, sus**, or **de Usted**. Both **su** and **de Usted** may be used.

Ex.—su libro,   ⎫   sus casas,   ⎫
  el libro de V., ⎬ *your book.* las casas de V., ⎬ *your houses.*
  su libro de V.,   ⎭   sus casas de V., ⎭

98. The definite article is omitted, and the full form of the possessive follows the noun in the following cases :

(*a*) In certain familiar expressions.

Ex.—á casa nuestra,   *to our house.*
  á fe mía,   *on my word* (fe, *litt. faith*).

(*b*) In direct address, unless an adjective accompanies the noun.

Ex.—amigo mío,   *my friend.*
  querido amigo mío, ⎫
  mi querido amigo,   ⎬ *my dear friend.*
                ⎭

99. The possessive adjective should be repeated before every noun to which it applies.

Ex.—mi padre y mi madre,   *my father and mother.*

100. The possessive is replaced by the definite article :

(*a*) When the possessor is clearly indicated.

Ex.—La niña baja la cabeza,   *The girl bows her head.*
  Ha perdido el brazo,   *He has lost his arm.*

(*b*) When the name of the thing possessed is the direct object of a verb, possession then being expressed by a personal pronoun in the dative.

Ex.—Me corto el dedo,   *I cut my finger.*
  Le tomo la mano,   *I take his (her) hand.*

Possessive Pronouns

101. The possessive pronouns are used instead of, not with, a noun. They are formed by placing the definite article before the full possessive adjective **mío, tuyo, suyo**, etc.

Ex.—su casa y la mía,   *his house and mine.*
  nuestros amigos y los vuestros,   *our friends and yours.*
  mi pluma y la suya (*or* la de V., § 97),   *my pen and yours.*

102. The neuter article, **lo**, when preceding a possessive, refers to some indefinite thing possessed.

Ex.—lo mío,   *mine, what is mine.*
  lo tuyo,   *thine, what is thine.*

EXERCISE IX.

VOCABULARY IX.

(Words given in preceding Chapter.)

A. 1. La pluma de oro es de V. 2. Mi vecino y la hija suya quieren ir á la ciudad. 3. ¿ Tiene V. su libro? He perdido el mío, y mi hermano el suyo. 4. Amigo mío ¿ quieres tú (quiere V.) ir al campo? Mi caballo y el tuyo (el suyo, el de V.) están aquí (*here*). 6. La culpa no es mía, sino de V. 7. El pobre soldado ha perdido los brazos en la guerra (*war*). 8. ¿Es el comerciante un primo de V.? Su casa de él es una de las mejores de la ciudad. 9. Mi hermano y mi hermana están á casa.

B. 1. I have a horse and my brother has one also[1]; his is better than mine. 2. The general has lost the battle[2]. 3. I have given the keys[3] to my friend, not to yours. 4. The boy cuts his finger with his father's knife. 5. His good parents and mine (and yours). 6. Your friends (*masc. and fem.*) and ours (and theirs). 7. Her houses and yours (and his). 8. We speak of our dear sisters and of yours. 9. His (her, your, their) house. 10. My house is near[4] hers.

[1] también. [2] la batalla. [3] See Ex. VIII, *A.* 1. [4] cerca de.

CHAPTER X.

DEMONSTRATIVES

Demonstrative Adjectives

103. The demonstrative adjectives agree in gender and number with the noun they determine. They are:

	Singular			Plural	
Masc.	*Fem.*		*Masc.*	*Fem.*	
este,	esta,	*this.*	estos,	estas,	*these.*
ese,	esa,	*that.*	esos,	esas,	*those.*
aquel,	aquella,	*that.*	aquellos,	aquellas,	*those.*

Before **otro**, *other*, **este** and **ese** become **estotro** and **esotro**, and are regularly inflected.

104. **Este** signifies what is near the speaker; **ese** what is near the person spoken to, and **aquel**, what is remote from both. In reference to time, **este** indicates the present time, **ese**, a near period, and **aquel**, a remote time.

Ex.—este libro, *this book* (*by me*); este año, *this year.*
esa silla, *that chair* (*by you*); esos años, *those years.*
aquel río, *that river* (*yonder*); aquel siglo, *that century.*

105. The demonstrative adjectives regularly precede their noun (*Cf.* **Ex.** above). They may be found after the noun in certain expressions, to denote emphasis, anger, or contempt.

Ex.—el hombre este, "*this*" man. el pícaro ese, *that rogue.*

106. In business letters, the words **ciudad**, *city*, **plaza**, *place*, *market*, are usually omitted after **esta**, **esa**, and **aquella**.

Ex.—Llegué á esta, *I arrived here (in the city where I am).*
Iré á esa, *I shall go to that city (where you are).*
Salió de aquella, *He left that city (another city).*

Demonstrative Pronouns

107. The demonstrative pronouns have the same form as the demonstrative adjectives. They are used in place of a noun with which they agree in gender and number, and they assume the written accent-mark (´) to distinguish them from the adjectives.

Ex.—este libro y aquél, *this book and that one.*
aquellos caballeros y *those gentlemen (yonder), and*
ésos, *those (by you).*

108. To the forms given above must be added the neuter pronouns **esto, eso, aquello**, which refer to a statement, an abstract idea, never to a definite noun.

Ex.—Ha leído V. esto? *Have you read this?*
Eso es cierto. *That is certain.*

109. The English demonstrative *this* (*that*, etc.), when followed by *of*, is rendered in Spanish by the definite article which agrees with the noun already mentioned.

Ex.—mis libros y los de mi *my books and those of my*
amigo, *friend (or my friend's).*
su casa y la de su *your house and that of your*
tío, *uncle.*

EXERCISE X.

VOCABULARY X.

(Words given in preceding Chapter.)

A. 1. Este vino es de Madeira, ése de Jerez y aquél de Málaga. 2. Ese muchacho es bueno, es mejor que aquél.

3. ¿ Quiere V. aquellas naranjas ó ésas ?   4. Son las ocho y media, y el mozo (*waiter*) ese no me ha dado mi café. 5. Tengo este libro y el de mi hermano.   6. No tengo mi fusil, sino (*but*) el de mi amigo.   7. Llegué á esta á las nueve é iré á esa á las diez.   8. Este comerciante dice que no tiene dinero; eso es imposible.

B. 1. These pens are better than those, but my friend's are the best.   2. My father has given me this book and that one.   3. Those gentlemen and those [1] are neighbors of mine.   4. He speaks of that beautiful Spanish city; I want to see it.   5. Those two boys are brothers; this one is a [2] sailor, that one is a [2] soldier.   6. This chair is more comfortable [3] than yours; do you want it ?   7. Have you read this ?   I have not read it.   8. We speak of these gardens and of those of your neighbor.   9. This is new, but that is certain.

[1] yonder.   [2] See § 17 a.   [3] cómoda.

CHAPTER XI.

RELATIVES

110. The relative pronouns are: **que** (invariable), *who, which, that;* **quien** (*plur.* **quienes**), *who;* **el** (**la** or **lo**) **cual, los** (or **las**) **cuales**, *who, which;* **el que** (article inflected), *who, which,* and the relative possessive **cuyo**, *whose, of which,* inflected like an adjective in **o**.

111. All relatives (except **cuyo**), agree as far as inflected with their antecedents.

112. In Spanish, the relative pronoun is never omitted nor can it be separated from a governing preposition. Expressions like: *The man I saw; the house he speaks of,* must be rendered by: *The man whom I saw; the house of which he speaks.*

Que

113. **Que** is the most common relative, since it can be used as subject or object and for persons and things. After a preposition, however, it can be used only for things. It should follow its antecedent immediately.

Ex.—el hombre que viene,   *the man who comes.*
    los hombres que vienen,   *the men who come.*
    la mujer que ví,   *the woman that I saw.*
    la carta que está en casa,   *the letter which is at home.*
    los asuntos de que hablamos, *the affairs of which we speak.*

Quien

114. **Quien** refers only to persons or personified things, and takes the place of **que** after a preposition.

Ex.—Los hombres de quienes hablamos no han llegado, *The men of whom we speak have not arrived.*

la señora á* quien ví ayer, *the lady that I saw yesterday.*

115. Quien is rarely used as subject unless it includes its antecedent, in which case it means *he who (those who), any one who.* . . .

Ex.—Quien poco tiene, poco teme, *He who has little, fears little.*

Habla á quien quiere escucharle, *He speaks to any one who will hear him.*

La verdad es amarga; quien te la dice te estima, *Truth is bitter; he who says it to thee esteems thee.*

116. Quien requires **á** in the personal accusative case while **que** does not.*

Ex.—el hombre que veo,
el hombre á quien veo, } *the man that I see.*

El cual, El que

117. El cual and **el que** are more precise relatives than **que** and **quien**, indicating, as they do by their inflection, the gender and number of the antecedent. They apply to both persons and things, and are used instead of **que** and **quien** in the following cases:

(*a*) To prevent ambiguity when the pronoun is separated from the antecedent by another noun.†

* Spanish usually requires the preposition *á* before a direct object denoting a person or personified thing. See § **234.**

† If the nouns are of same gender and number, a different construction is necessary, or the noun should be repeated.

Ex.—He visto á la hermana
de mi amigo, la cual
está enferma,

*I have seen my friend's sister who
is ill.*

Es un correo despacha-
do por la reina, el cual
nos trae buenas no-
ticias,

*He is a messenger sent by the queen,
who brings us good news.*

(*b*) To continue a clause having a complete sense, the pronoun following a pause or mark of punctuation.

Ex.—Compré ayer un libro
muy curioso, el cual
yo no había leído
nunca,

*Yesterday I bought a very curious
book which I had never read.*

118. After a long preposition, **el cual** or **el que** is preferable
to **que**, which is generally used only after monosyllables.

Ex.—la casa en que vivo,

the house in which I live.

la casa cerca de la cual
hay una fuente,

*the house near which there is a
fountain.*

119. The English expressions: *he who, she who,* etc., also
which, those which, are rendered in Spanish by **el que** or
aquel que, and their variations (rarely by **quien** when speaking of persons. *Cf.* § **115**).

Ex.—El que habla es mi
primo,

He who speaks is my cousin.

mis libros y los (*or*
aquellos) que están
sobre la mesa,

*my books and those which are on
the table.*

Los que salen son nues-
tros vecinos,

*Those who are going out are our
neighbors.*

120. Lo cual and **lo que** refer to an idea or a statement,
never to a definite noun.

Ex.—Lo que dice no me gusta,

What he says does not please me.

Dicho lo cual, salió,

Saying which, he went out.

121. Donde, *where,* is often used as a relative of place.

Ex.—la casa donde (*or* en que,   *the house in which he lives.*
    or en la cual) vive,

Cuyo

122. Cuyo, is a relative indicating possession, and corresponding to the English *whose, of which.* It refers to persons and things, but like a possessive adjective agrees with the object possessed, and not with the possessor. It might be called the genitive or possessive case of **que.**

Ex.—El caballero á cuya hija   *The gentleman to whose daughter*
    le he presentado á V.,   *I presented you is my neighbor.*
    es mi vecino,
    un pueblo, cuyo nombre   *a village, the name of which I wish*
    quiero olvidar,   *to forget.*

EXERCISE XI.

VOCABULARY XI.

todavía, *yet, still.*   ahora, *now.*   ayer, *yesterday.*

(Also words given in preceding Chapter.)

A. 1. Lo que V. dice es verdadero, pero no es nuevo. 2. Los soldados que han llegado ayer están todavía en la ciudad. 3. La casa cerca de la cual hay una fuente es la del comerciante. 4. La señora á quien ví ayer es hermana del juez. 5. El caballero á cuya hermana he mandado flores es amigo de mi padre. 6. Tengo una casa de campo en la cual he pasado los mejores años de mi vida (*life*). 7. El hombre que viene y de quien hablamos es amigo mío.

B. 1. The books which I bought yesterday have not yet arrived.   2. He who has money is not always happy.
3. My friend's horse is not very good; he fears to go to the city with it.   4. The boys to whom he gives oranges and pears[1] are the merchant's sons.   5. The affairs of which they speak are very important[2].   6. Have you seen[3] the messenger who brings letters from[4] the soldiers?   7. What he says is not true; I do not believe it.   8. The oranges which I bought are on[5] the table; have you seen them?
9. The friends in whose house I live are in Madrid.   10. The house I bought yesterday is larger than the one I have now.

[1] the pear, la pera.   [2] importante.   [3] Insert *á*.   [4] de.   [5] sobre.

CHAPTER XII.

INTERROGATIVES

123. The interrogative pronouns are: **qué?** *what?* **quién?** (*plur.* **quiénes**) *who?* **cuál?** (*plur.* **cuáles**) *which? what?* **cúyo?** (**–a, –os, –as**) *whose?* They take the accent-mark to distinguish them from the relatives. All are used (except **quién**) as interrogative adjectives, immediately preceding the noun.

124. Qué may precede nouns representing persons or things, or it may be used alone.

Ex.—¿ Qué hombre es éste?   *What man is this?*
¿ Qué noticias trae?   *What news does he bring?*
¿ Qué decía él?   *What did he say?*
¿ De qué habla V.?   *Of what are you speaking?*

125. Qué is also employed in exclamations, with the meaning of *what!* . . . (or *how!* . . . before an adjective).

Ex.—¡ Qué desdicha!   *What a misfortune!*
¡ Qué vista grandiosa!   *What a magnificent view!*
¡ Qué hermosa es!   *How beautiful she is!*

126. Quién can only refer to persons, and is never connected with a noun.

Ex.—¿ Quién es?   *Who is it?*
¿ Quiénes son?   *Who are they?*
¿ De quién habla V.?   *Of whom do you speak?*

127. Cuál (*plur.* **cuáles**) is the pronoun used when the person addressed is requested to single out of a number, one or more persons or things.

Ex.—Aquí están los caballos ¿ cuál es el suyo ?	*Here are the horses, which is yours ?*
¿ Cuál de los libros quiere V. ?	*Which of the books do you want ?*
¿ Cuáles de sus amigos han venido ?	*Which of his friends have come ?*

128. Cúyo is rarely used as interrogative except before the verb *to be*. It agrees with the noun possessed.

Ex.—¿ Cúyo es este sombrero ?	*Whose hat is this ?*
¿ Cúya es la casa aquella ?	*Whose house is that ?*

EXERCISE XII.

VOCABULARY XII.

(Words given in preceding Chapter.)

A. 1. ¿ Qué hora es ? 2. ¿ Qué (cosa) quiere él ? 3. ¿ Á cuál de sus amigos de V. habla el señor juez ? 4. ¿ Cúyas son esas cartas ? 5. Quién se las ha mandado á V. ? 6. ¿ De quién (cúyo) es este sombrero ? 7. ¿ Qué decía su hermano de V. ? 8. Aquí están los libros; ¿ cuáles son los suyos, éstos, ó aquéllos ? 9. ¿ Ha visto V. el palacio del rey ? ¡ Qué hermoso es !

B. 1. Who is it ? 2. What is it ? 3. What does he speak of ? 4. Who is the author of this book ? 5. Whose[1] house is that ? It is the merchant's. 6. Of which letter do you speak ? 7. What do you say of these flowers ? 8. Which of these houses is his ? 9. What is the date[2] of his letter ? 10. How happy you are ! 11. Whose horses are these ? Which (ones) are yours ? 12. What is the news[3] in yesterday's paper[4] ?

---

[1] Translate in two ways. [2] fecha (*fem.*) [3] Translate *What news brings. . . .* [4] periódico (*masc.*)

CHAPTER XIII.

INDEFINITES

129. Under this title will be included several words which are employed sometimes as adjectives, sometimes as pronouns, and occasionally as adverbs, all more or less indefinite in meaning.

Alguien, Algo, Alguno

130. Alguien, *somebody, anybody*, **algo**, *something, anything*, are invariable, and used only as pronouns. **Alguien** refers to persons only, **algo** to things only. They cannot be used in negative sentences. (See § **134.**)

Ex.—Alguien llama,	*Somebody calls.*
¿ Ha encontrado V. á alguien ?	*Have you met anybody ?*
Hallé algo en el patio,	*I found something in the yard.*
¿ Busca V. algo ?	*Are you looking for anything ?*

131. Before an adjective, **algo** is used adverbially, and means *somewhat*.

Ex.—Este libro es algo caro, *This book is somewhat dear.*

132. Alguno is varied like any adjective in **o**. It applies both to persons and things. Used with a noun it means *some, any, a few*, and loses the final **o** before a masculine singular. (See § **42.**)

Ex.—algún hombre, *some man.* alguna niña, *some girl.*
algunos buques, *a few ships.*

133. As a pronoun, **alguno** means *somebody, something,* *some*, etc.   It replaces **alguien** when applied to one of a number of persons referred to or thought of, and may be followed by **de**.

Ex.—alguno de ellos (not alguien de ellos),	*some one of them.*
¿ Ha llegado alguien ?	*Has anybody come?*
¿ Ha llegado alguno ?	*Has anyone come? (of those we expect).*
Vende naranjas; quiero comprar algunas,	*He sells oranges; I wish to buy some (a few).*

Nadie, Nada, Ninguno

134. **Nadie***, nobody, no one,* **nada***, nothing,* **ninguno***, no one, none, no . . .* are the negative forms of **alguien, algo, alguno**; they follow the rules given above but require the addition of **no** when they stand after the verb (not when preceding it, or used alone).

Ex.—Nadie está contento con su suerte,	*No one is satisfied with his fate.*
No hallé nada en el patio (*or* nada hallé en el patio),	*I found nothing in the yard.*
ningún hombre,	*no man.*
ninguna casa,	*no house.*
ningún de ellos (*not* nadie de ellos),	*no one of them.*
No tengo ningún libro,	*I have no book.*

135. By exception, **alguno** can be used in a negative sentence, or after **sin**, *without,* but it always follows the noun which must be singular.   It has then the meaning of the English *any*.

Ex.—No tengo libro alguno,	*I have not any book.*
sin duda alguna,	*without any doubt.*

136. Cada, *each, every,* is invariable, and when used as an adjective precedes the noun. Used without a noun, **un–o (–a)**, and **cual** are added to **cada**.

Ex.—cada muchacho,	*each boy.*
cada pluma,	*each pen.*
Cada uno tiene sus asuntos,	*Each one has his affairs.*
Cada una de las damas lleva su abanico,	*Each (one) of the ladies carries her fan.*

137. **Un–o (–a, –os, –as)**, when an indefinite pronoun, means *one, some one, any one,* and in the plural *some*. It is often contrasted or combined with **otro**, *other.*

Ex.—No está uno siempre dichoso,	*One is not always happy.*
¿Puede uno ver lo que pasa?	*Can one see what happens?*
Uno va y otro viene,	*One goes and another comes.*

Note the combinations : **uno y otro**, *both ;* **uno ú otro**, *either ;* **ni uno ni otro**, *neither.*

138. **Todo**, as an adjective, precedes the noun and means : *all, the whole, every.*

Ex.—Trabaja todo el día,	*He works all day.*
Pedro gasta todo su dinero,	*Peter wastes all his money.*
Todo hombre honrado le respeta,	*Every honorable man respects him.*
Viene todos los días,	*He comes every day.*

139. As a pronoun, **todo** is used in the singular with the meaning of *all, everything ;* in the plural it applies to persons and things, and varies accordingly.

Ex.—En esta tienda hay un poco de todo,	*In this shop there is a little of everything.*

Todo es vanidad en este mundo, — *All is vanity in this world.*

Todos están perdidos, — *All (masc.) are lost.*

Las he visto á todas, — *I have seen them all (fem.).*

140. Following is a list of some other indefinite adjectives and pronouns :

Cualquiera*, *Any, whatever, whichever.*

Ex.—cualquier país, — *whatever country.*

Eso lo sabe cualquiera, — *Any one knows this.*

Quienquiera, *Whoever, anyone.*

Ex.—quienquiera que lo diga, — *whoever may say it.*

Tal† (*plur.* **tales**), *Such a, such.*

Ex.—tal hombre, — *such a man.*

tales días, — *such days.*

He visto á un tal, — *I have seen such a one.*

Mismo, *Same, self.*

Ex.—el mismo día, — *the same day.*

el día mismo, — *the day itself, the very day.*

Han hecho lo mismo, — *They have done the same (thing).*

Fulan–o (–a), *So and so, such a one.*

Ex.—Me lo ha dicho fulano, — *So and so has said it to me.*

Zutano, **Mengano**, **Perengano**, are words similar to **Fulano**, employed to indicate persons whose names are not recollected or intentionally not to be mentioned. They can be rendered by : *so and so, such a one, Mr. Blank*, etc.

---

* *Cualquiera* (*pl. cualesquiera*) may drop the *a* when *immediately* preceding the noun. *Cualesquier noticias*, Whatever news.

† ¿ *Qué tal ?* is frequently used in the sense of : How do you do ?

EXERCISE XIII.

VOCABULARY XIII.

(Words given in preceding Chapter.)

A. 1. Voy á comprar algunos libros.   2. Nadie habla (no habla nadie) de aquel asunto.   3. Ninguno de mis amigos está aquí ; no ha llegado ninguno de ellos.   4. Quiero comprar algo ¿qué vende V.?   Tengo naranjas y manzanas ¿quiere V. algunas?   5. No quiero ningunas, son algo caras.   6. Cada país tiene su lengua y sus costumbres (*customs*).   7. Ninguna casa de la ciudad es tan hermosa como el palacio del conde.   8. En esta tienda hay un poco de todo, y todo lo que hay es bueno.   9. No dice nada á nadie.

B. 1. I have no oranges but my brother has some.   2. Are you looking for[1] anything? No; I do not want anything.   3. I have seen some one who is looking for[1] you.   4. He spends all his money without buying[2] anything useful.   5. Who calls? Nobody.   6. Which (one) of them speaks? No one.   7. Here are the pens; I do not want them, I have others.   8. The same (thing[3]) happens every day.   9. I have, says the King, a[3] hundred other generals as good as he.   10. Each (one) of the girls has a flower in her[4] hand.   11. Such books are very useful for the young[5].   12. Any pen is better than no pen.

[1] Translate *to look for* by one word.   [2] comprar.   [3] Omit.   See § **46**.   [4] See § **100** (*a*).   [5] los jóvenes.

CHAPTER XIV.

THE VERB ; THE AUXILIARY "HABER"

141. The auxiliaries most used in Spanish are: **haber**, *to have ; * **ser**, *to be ; * **estar**, *to be*. Although they are all irregular, their conjugation will be given before that of the regular verbs as they serve to form all the compound tenses.

NOTE.—The conjugation of these auxiliaries should be thoroughly mastered by the student, as it will greatly facilitate the study of regular and irregular verbs. For the proper handling of the spoken language, and for an accurate understanding of the written language, a thorough knowledge of verb forms is *absolutely* necessary.

The auxiliary "Haber"

142. **Haber**, *To have*, is used only as an auxiliary ; *to have*, meaning *to possess*, is expressed by **tener**. (See § **216**.)

CONJUGATION

Infinitive: **haber**, *to have*. Present participle * : **habiendo**, *having*. Past Participle : **habido**, *had*.

Present Indicative	Present Subjunctive
Yo† he, *I have*, etc.	haya, *I may have*‡, etc.
Tú has	hayas
Él (ella, V.) ha	haya
Nosotros hemos	hayamos
Vosotros habéis	hayáis
Ellos (ellas, V.V.) han	hayan

* Really: *Gerund;* this name will be used as it is more familiar. See §**271**.
† Pronouns will hereafter be omitted.
‡ The Spanish subjunctive is variously rendered in English according to context.

Imperfect Indicative

hab ía,   *I had*, etc.
hab ías
hab ía
hab íamos
hab íais
hab ían

Future Indicative

habr é,   *I shall have*, etc.
habr ás
habr á
habr emos
habr éis
habr án

Present Conditional

habr ía,   *I should have*, etc.
habr ías
habr ía

habr íamos,   *We should have*, etc.
habr íais
habr ían

Preterit

hub e,   *I had*, etc.
hubist e
hub o
hub imos
hub isteis
hub ieron

Imperfect Subjunctive

hub iera,   *I might have**, etc.
hub ieras
hub iera
hub iéramos
hub ierais
hub ieran

2d Imperfect Subjunctive

hub iese,   *I might have*, etc.
hub ieses
hub iese
hub iésemos
hub ieseis
hub iesen

Future Subjunctive

hub iere,   *I should have**, etc.
hub ieres
hub iere
hub iéremos
hub iereis
hub ieren

Imperative

Wanting.

143. The past participle when conjugated with **haber** remains always invariable. When used with any other verb, or when no verb is expressed the participle, like an adjective, agrees in gender and number with the noun which it modifies.

Ex.—He escrito la carta,   *I have written the letter.*
La carta está mal escrita,   *The letter is badly written.*

* See foot note on page 60.

144. Haber followed by **de** and an infinitive has the meaning of : *to have to, to be to,* etc.

Ex.—¿ Qué había de hacer él? *What was he to do?*

Hemos de comer á las seis. *We are to dine at six o'clock.*

145. Haber, used impersonally means : *there is, there are; there was,* etc. Only the 3d person singular, the infinitive and participles can be used thus ; the 3d person singular of the Present Indicative becomes **hay** (**ha** after a measure of time). As an impersonal **haber** builds its own tenses : **ha habido, había habido,** etc.

Ex.—Hay buenas noticias en   *There is good news in the paper.*
    el periódico,

Habrá mucha lluvia este   *There will be much rain this year.*
    año,

Ha habido ocasiones de   *There have been occasions of great*
    mucho interés,   *interest.* (Lit. *much interest.*)

tres años ha,   *three years ago.*

146. Haber * impersonal when followed by **que** and an infinitive, denotes obligation, necessity, and may be translated by : *to be necessary.*

Ex.—Hay que perdonarle,   *It is necessary to forgive him.*

  ¿ Qué hay que hacer?   *What is to be done?*

EXERCISE XIV.

VOCABULARY XIV.

ahora,   *now.*

(Also words given in preceding Chapter.)

A. 1. Habíamos, habremos, habríamos. 2. Hubo, habrá, ha, hay. 3. Hayan, han, hubieron, hubieran, hubiesen.

* *Tener que,* before an infinitive indicates also obligation, necessity, etc. It is stronger than *Haber que* . . .

4. He, hube, habré, habría, había, hubiera, hubiese. 5. El padre ha dado una manzana á su hijo. 6. ¿ Han llegado los libros? Voy á ver ahora si han llegado. 7. He dado mi sombrero viejo al pobre muchacho. 8. Dice que me ha mandado una carta, pero no ha llegado todavía. 9. ¿ Habrá guerra ó no la habrá? 10. Hay más de tres mil quinientas millas (*miles*) de Nueva York á Barcelona. 11. Hemos de hacer un viaje por la mar. 12. Hay mucho que ver en esta ciudad, pero no tenemos tiempo.

B. 1. I have written a letter to my brother who is now in France. 2. We have bought apples and oranges. 3. Have your friends arrived? No, sir, they have not yet arrived. 4. I have spent* six months in France, and I have learned the French language. 5. Our neighbor is to dine with us this evening at seven o'clock. 6. There are broad streets and beautiful squares in this city. 7. Had you spoken to this man? I had spoken to him two or three times. 8. There were more than two hundred soldiers in the street. 9. There has been a great battle in this war. 10. What were we to do?

* Words not already given are to be found in the general vocabularies at the end of the book.

CHAPTER XV.

THE AUXILIARIES "SER" AND "ESTAR"

The Auxiliary "Ser"

147. The passive construction is formed by the auxiliary **ser**, *to be*, and the past participle of the verb conjugated.

CONJUGATION

Infinitive: **ser**, *to be*. Present participle: **siendo**, *being*. Past participle: **sido**, *been*.

Present Indicative	Present Subjunctive
soy,　*I am*, etc.	sea (Gen. *I may* [1] *be*), etc.
eres	seas
es	sea
somos	seamos
sois	seáis
son	sean

Imperfect Indicative	Future Indicative	Present Conditional
era,　*I was*, etc.	ser é, *I shall be*, etc.	ser ía,　*I should be*, etc.
eras	ser ás	ser ías
era	ser á	ser ía
éramos	ser emos	ser íamos
erais	ser éis	ser íais
eran	ser án	ser ían

Preterit	Imperfect Subjunctive
fuí,　*I was*, etc.	fuera,　*I might* [1] *be*, etc.
fuiste	fueras
fué	fuera
fuimos	fuéramos
fuisteis	fuerais
fueron	fueran

[1] Variously rendered in English according to context.

2d Imperfect Subjunctive	**Future Subjunctive**
fuese, *I might* [1] *be*, etc.	fuere, *I should* [1] *be*, etc.
fueses	fueres
fuese	fuere
fuésemos	fuéremos
fueseis	fuereis
fuesen	fueren

Imperative

sé, *be (thou)*.   sed, *be (ye)*.

NOTE.—The imperative has only two persons : *2d sing.* and *2d plur.* Other persons, and *all* negative imperatives, are expressed by corresponding forms of the *Present Subjunctive.*

Ex.—Sean ellos,   *Let them be.*
         No seas tonto,   *Do not be foolish (2d sing.)*

148. The compound tenses of **ser** are all formed by means of the auxiliary **haber**, as : **he sido**, *I have been ;* **habré sido**, *I shall have been ;* **haber sido**, *to have been*, etc.

149. The past participle used with **ser** agrees in gender and number with the subject of the verb.   (*Cf.* § **143**.)

The Auxiliary " Estar "

150. Estar, *To be*, is employed with the *Present Participle* (*Gerund*), to form the progressive construction as in English : *I am working*, **estoy trabajando**.

CONJUGATION

Infinitive : **estar**, *to be*.   Present Participle : **estando**, *being*. Past Participle : **estado**, *been*.

Present Indicative	**Present Subjunctive**
estoy, *I am*, etc.	esté, *I may* [1] *be*, etc.
estás	estés

[1] Variously rendered in English according to context.

Present Indicative	Present Subjunctive
está	esté
estamos	estemos
estáis	estéis
están	estén

Imperfect Indicative	Future Indicative	Present Conditional
est aba, *I was*, etc.	estar é, *I shall be*, etc.	estar ía, *I should be*,
est abas	estar ás	estar ías [etc.
est aba	estar á	estar ía
est ábamos	estar emos	estar íamos
est abais	estar éis	estar íais
est aban	estar án	estar ían

Preterit	Imperfect Subjunctive
estuv e, *I was*, etc.	estuv iera, *I might*[1] *be*, etc.
estuv iste	estuv ieras
estuv o	estuv iera
estuv imos	estuv iéramos
estuv isteis	estuv ierais
estuv ieron	estuv ieran

2d Imperfect Subjunctive	Future Subjunctive
estuv iese, *I might*[1] *be*, etc.	estuv iere, *I should*[1] *be*, etc.
estuv ieses	estuv ieres
estuv iese	estuv iere
estuv iésemos	estuv iéremos
estuv ieseis	estuv iereis
estuv iesen	estuv ieren

Imperative

está, *be* (*thou*).   estad, *be* (*ye*).

(*Cf.* above note, § 147.)

151. Ser and **estar**, although both meaning *to be*, are not interchangeable. **Ser** expresses what is inherent or permanent, while **estar** is applied to what is accidental or temporary*.

[1] Variously rendered in English according to context.

* Note the following expressions : *ser bueno*, to be good ; *estar bueno*, to be well ; *ser malo*, to be bad ; *estar malo*, to be ill.

Ex.—Es español,	*He is a Spaniard.*
El español está en Fran-cia,	*The Spaniard is in France.*
Este libro ha sido tradu-cido,	*This book has been translated.*
Este libro está mal tra-ducido,	*This book is poorly translated.*
El hielo es frío,	*Ice is cold.*
El agua está fría,	*Water is cold.*

Estar (from Latin *stare*, to stand) is also used to indicate the position, location, situation of a person or thing whether it be permanent or not.

Ex.—La casa del comerciante está en el campo,	*The house of the merchant is in the country.*
Madrid está á orillas del Manzanares,	*Madrid is on the banks of the Man-zanares.*
La puerta está abierta,	*The door stands open.*
Mi primo está en casa,	*My cousin is at home.*

152. The past participles **sido** and **estado** are always conjugated with **haber**, and therefore never vary.

EXERCISE XV.

VOCABULARY XV.

Conjugations of *ser* and *estar*.

(Also words given in preceding Chapter; words not given are to be found in general vocabulary.)

A. 1. Será, sería, seré, seremos, serían. 2. Fué, fuera, fuese, fuí, fueron, fuimos. 3. Era, éramos, somos, seamos, sea, sé, sido. 4. Estuvo, estuviéramos, estuve, estaba, estaré,

estaría. 5. Está, esté, estoy, están, estado. 6. Esos niños
son amados porque son buenos. 7. Hemos estado ya en la
casa de nuestros amigos. 8. El descuido del general ha
sido fatal al regimiento. 9. Mi primo está trabajando.
10. Francia es una república. 11. Los enemigos de la
patria han sido vencidos. 12. ¿ Cómo está V., señor juez ?

B. 1. The letter has not been written by[1] him. 2. It is
impossible to see the judge now; he is working. 3. The
water of this river is as cold as ice. 4. My cousin was in
the city the other day; he is now in the country. 5. What
is the distance from New York to Havana ? 6. How is your
neighbor's son ? He is not well. 7. These men have been
very happy, but now they are not[2]. 8. What are you looking for ? My penknife. It is in the table-drawer. 9. The
house of the merchant is on[3] Fifth avenue. 10. The
soldiers who have arrived are still in[4] town.

[1] por. [2] Insert: *it*. [3] en la . . . [4] Translate *in the town*.

CHAPTER XVI.

CONJUGATION OF THE REGULAR VERBS

153. All Spanish verbs in the infinitive end in –ar, –er, or –ir, and are accordingly divided into three classes or conjugations.

Ex.—hablar,	*to speak,*	1st conjugation.
vender,	*to sell,*	2d "
vivir,	*to live,*	3d "

154. The stem of a verb is obtained by removing the infinitive ending; thus **habl–, vend–, viv–,** are the stems of the above verbs.

155. The simple tenses of a Spanish verb can be obtained by making regular changes from three forms called principal parts. These are: the Infinitive, the Present Indicative, and the Preterit.

156.   **TABLE OF TENSE FORMATION**

From the Infinitive:

Future Indicative		**Present Conditional**	
Infinitive + é		*Infinitive* + ía
"	ás	"	ías
"	á	"	ía
"	emos	"	íamos
"	éis	"	íais
"	án	"	ían

Imperfect Indicative

	1st conj.	2d and 3d conj.
Infinitive stem +	aba	ía
"	abas	ías
"	aba	ía
"	ábamos	íamos
"	abais	íais
"	aban	ían

Imperative

2d person plural by changing final *r* to *d*.

From the Present Indicative:

Present Subjunctive

	1st conj.	2d and 3d conj.
Change *o* of 1st pers. sing. to :	e	a
	es	as
	e	a
	emos	amos
	éis	áis
	en	an

Imperative

The 2d pers. sing. of the Imperative is the same as the 3d pers. sing. of the Present Indicative. Other persons (except 2d plur.) and negatives taken from Pres. Subj.

From the Preterit:

Change *ron* of 3d pers. plur. of the Preterit to:

Imperfect Subj.	2d Imperfect Subj.	Future Subjunctive
ra	se	re
ras	ses	res
ra	se	re
'–ramos	'–semos	'–remos
rais	seis	reis
ran	sen	ren

Note.—This formation of tenses, while not exactly scientific, is believed to be more easily understood, and of more general application *.

* It may also help the student to note that the 1st and 3d persons sing. *always* end in a vowel, the 1st plural *always* ends in *–mos*, and the 3d plural in *–n*.

157. According to the formation given above, the model verbs of the three conjugations are inflected as follows :

FIRST CONJUGATION

Hablar, *to speak.*

Infinitive : **habl ar**, *to speak.* Present Participle : **habl an do**, *speaking.* Past Participle : **habl ado**, *spoken.*

From the Infinitive :

Future Indicative	Present Conditional
hablar *é*, *I shall speak*, etc.	**hablar** *ía*, *I should speak*, etc.
hablar *ás*	hablar *ías*
hablar *á*	hablar *ía*
hablar *emos*	hablar *íamos*
hablar *éis*	hablar *íais*
hablar *án*	hablar *ían*

Imperfect Indicative	Imperative
habl *aba*, *I spoke*, etc.	2d person plural :
habl *abas*	habl a**d**, *speak (ye).*
habl *aba*	
habl *ábamos*	
habl *abais*	
habl *aban*	

From the Present Indicative :

Present Indicative	Present Subjunctive	Imperative
habl **o**, *I speak.* etc.	habl *e*, *I may speak*[1], etc.	2d person singular :
habl *as*	habl *es*	gular :
habl *a*	habl *e*	habla, *speak (thou).*
habl *amos*	habl *emos*	
habl *áis*	habl *éis*	
habl *an*	habl *en*	

[1] Variously rendered in English according to context.

From the Preterit:

Preterit	Imperfect Subjunctive
habl *é,* *I spoke,* etc.	habl *ara,* *I might speak*[1], etc.
habl *aste*	habl *aras*
habl *ó*	habl *ara*
habl *amos*	habl *áramos*
habl *asteis*	habl *arais*
habl *aron*	habl *aran*

2d Imperfect Subjunctive	Future Subjunctive
habl *ase,* *I might speak*[1], etc.	habl *are,* *I should speak*[1], etc.
habl *ases*	habl *ares*
habl *ase*	habl *are*
habl *ásemos*	habl *áremos*
habl *aseis*	habl *areis*
habl *asen*	habl *aren*

158.   SECOND CONJUGATION

Vender,   *to sell.*

Infinitive: **vend er,** *to sell.*   Present Participle: **vend iendo,** *selling.*   Past Participle: **vend ido,** *sold.*

From the Infinitive:

Future Indicative	Present Conditional
vender *é,* *I shall sell,* etc.	**vender** *ía,* *I should sell,* etc.
vender *ás*	vender *ías*
vender *á*	vender *ía*
vender *emos*	vender *íamos*
vender *éis*	vender *íais*
vender *án*	vender *ían*

Imperfect Indicative		Imperative
vend *ía,* *I sold,* etc.	vend *íamos*	2d person plural:
vend *ías*	vend *íais*	**vend ed,** *sell (ye).*
vend *ía*	vend *ían*	

[1] Variously rendered in English according to context.

From the Present Indicative:

Present Indicative	Present Subjunctive	Imperative
vend **o**, *I sell*, etc.	vend *a*, *I may sell* [1], etc.	2d person singular :
vend *es*	vend *as*	vend *e*, *sell* (*thou*).
vend *e*	vend *a*	
vend *emos*	vend *amos*	
vend *éis*	vend *áis*	
vend *en*	vend *an*	

From the Preterit:

Preterit	Imperfect Subjunctive
vend *i*, *I sold*, etc.	vend *iera*, *I might sell* [1], etc.
vend *iste*	vend *ieras*
vend *ió*	vend *iera*
vend *imos*	vend *iéramos*
vend *isteis*	vend *ierais*
vend *ieron*	vend *ieran*

2d Imperfect Subjunctive	Future Subjunctive
vend *iese*, *I might sell* [1], etc.	vend *iere*, *I should sell* [1], etc.
vend *ieses*	vend *ieres*
vend *iese*	vend *iere*
vend *iésemos*	vend *iéremos*
vend *ieseis*	vend *iereis*
vend *iesen*	vend *ieren*

159. THIRD CONJUGATION

Vivir, *to live.*

Infinitive : **viv ir**, *to live.* Present Participle : **viv iendo**, *living.* Past Participle : **viv ido**, *lived.*

[1] Variously rendered in English according to context.

From the Infinitive:

Future Indicative

vivir *é*, *I shall live*, etc.
vivir *ás*
vivir *á*
vivir *emos*
vivir *éis*
vivir *án*

Present Conditional

vivir *ía*, *I should live*, etc.
vivir *ías*
vivir *ía*
vivir *íamos*
vivir *íais*
vivir *ían*

Imperfect Indicative

viv *ía*, *I lived*, etc.
viv *ías*
viv *ía*
viv *íamos*
viv *íais*
viv *ían*

Imperative

2d person plural:
viv **id**, *live (ye)*.

From the Present Indicative:

Present Indicative

viv **o**, *I live*, etc.
viv *es*
viv *e*
viv *imos*
viv *ís*
viv *en*

Present Subjunctive

viv *a*, *I may live*[1], etc.
viv *as*
viv *a*
viv *amos*
viv *áis*
viv *an*

Imperative

2d person singular:
viv *e*, *live (thou)*.

From the Preterit:

Preterit

viv *í*, *I lived*, etc.
viv *iste*
viv *ió*
viv *imos*
viv *isteis*
viv **ieron**

Imperfect Subjunctive

viv *iera*, *I might live*[1], etc.
viv *ieras*
viv *iera*
viv *iéramos*
viv *ierais*
viv *ieran*

[1] Variously rendered in English according to context.

2d Imperfect Subjunctive	Future Subjunctive
viv ie*se*, *I might live* *, etc.	viv ie*re*, *I should live* [1], *etc.*
viv ie*ses*	viv ie*res*
viv ie*se*	viv ie*re*
viv ié*semos*	viv ié*remos*
viv ie*seis*	viv ie*reis*
viv ie*sen*	viv ie*ren*

NOTE.—The 2d and 3d conjugations have exactly the same endings except in the Infinitive, 1st and 2d plural Present Indicative and 2d plural Imperative.

EXERCISE XVI.

VOCABULARY XVI.

a!abar,	*to praise.*	aprender,	*to learn.*	permitir,	*to permit.*
comprar,	*to buy.*	beber,	*to drink.*	recibir,	*to receive.*
engañar,	*to deceive.*	comer,	*to eat.*	sufrir,	*to suffer.*
hallar,	*to find.*	temer,	*to fear.*	escribir,	*to write,*
mandar,	*to send.*	ayer,	*yesterday.*	escrito,	*written* (ir-
tomar,	*to take.*	hoy,	*to-day.*		regular).

A. 1. Give the Present and Past Participles of the verbs contained in the vocabulary. 2. Write out, for each verb: (*a*) The 1st person singular of the Present Indicative and Present Subjunctive. (*b*) The 1st person plural of the Future Indicative and Present Conditional. (*c*) The 3d person singular and the 3d person plural of the Preterit. (*d*) The Imperative.

B. 1. Your friends have praised[1] my neighbor. 2. Are you learning the Spanish language? 3. The boy wants to buy a gun but his father does not allow it. 4. Do not

---

* Variously rendered in English according to context.

[1] Insert *d*.

speak[1] to that man and he will not deceive you.   5. Yesterday, we bought apples and oranges, and to-day we will send them to our friends.   6. He has not received any news from his father.   7. We have a house in the country, and we live there during the summer.   8. I fear that my brother may not receive[2] my letter.   9. Will you take[3] a cup of coffee with us?   10. I do not drink coffee but I will take a glass of water.   11. Do not deceive[4] others, and you[5] will not be deceived.   12. The merchant who wrote the letter which we received yesterday lives in New York.

[1] *Cf.* § **147** Note.   [2] (*pres. subj.*)   [3] Translate *Do you wish to take.*
[4] Insert *á.*   [5] Omit.

CHAPTER XVII.

ORTHOGRAPHIC CHANGES

160. The pronunciation which the verb-stem has in the Infinitive must be maintained throughout the conjugation. As certain consonants have a different pronunciation according to the letter which they precede, the following changes are necessary in applying the above rule for maintaining a uniform pronunciation:

161. Verbs ending in –car, –gar, –guar change respectively c to qu, g to gu, gu to gü before e. This occurs throughout in the Present Subjunctive, and in the 1st pers. sing. of the Preterit Indicative.

Ex.—		*Preterit* *1st pers.*	*Pres.* *Subj.*
tocar,	*to touch.*	toqué	toque, toques, etc.
pagar,	*to pay.*	pagué	pague, pagues, etc.
Averiguar,	*to ascertain.*	averigüé	averigüe, averigües, etc.

but : toco, tocas, etc., pago, pagaba, etc.

162. Verbs ending in ger, gir, change g to j before a or o. Those ending in guir and quir change gu to g, and qu to c before a or o.

Ex.—		*Pres. Ind.* *1st pers.*	*Pres.* *Subj.*
escoger,	*to choose.*	escojo escoges, etc.	escoja escojas, etc.
dirigir,	*to guide.*	dirijo diriges, etc.	dirija dirijas, etc.
distinguir,	*to distinguish.*	distingo distingues, etc.	distinga distingas, etc.
delinquir,	*to transgress to.*	delinco (–ques), etc.	delinca (–as), etc.

163. When the endings –cer, –cir, are preceded by a consonant, the c changes to z before a or o; when a vowel precedes, a z is added to the c before a or o.

Ex.—		Pres. Ind.	Pres. Subj.
vencer,	to conquer.	venzo, vences, etc.	venza, venzas, etc.
conocer,	to know, to be acquainted.	conozco conoces, etc.	conozca conozcas, etc.

(Except cocer, see § 186; decir, § 201; hacer, § 206.)

164. Spanish laws of orthography do not allow an unaccented i between two vowels, or a z before e or i (§ 6); therefore, in verb endings, when i is between two vowels and unaccented, it changes to y; and z changes to c before e or i.

Ex.—creer, to believe. Pres. Part. : creyendo (not creiendo), but : Imp. Ind. : creía, creías, etc.

rezar, to pray. Preterit: recé, rezaste, etc. Pres. Subj. : rece, reces, etc.

165. The double consonants ll, ñ, absorb the i of the diphthong ie and io when they occur in the conjugation.

Ex.—		Pres. Part.	Imperf. Subj.
bullir,	to boil.	bullendo (not bulliendo)	bullera bulleras, etc.
bruñir,	to burnish.	bruñendo (not bruñiendo)	bruñera bruñeras, etc.

EXERCISE XVII.

VOCABULARY XVII.

buscar, to seek, to look for.   proteger, to protect.   leer, to read. llegar, to arrive.   producir, to produce.

(Also verbs given in preceding Chapter.)

A. 1. Give the Participles, the Present Indicative, the Preterit of llegar, proteger, dirigir, conocer. 2. Write the

3d person singular and the 1st person plural of the Imperfect Indicative, Future Indicative and Present Subjunctive of **buscar, vencer, escoger, leer.** 3. Give the forms of **pagar, proteger, producir,** that suffer orthographic changes.

B. 1. I do not believe what he tells me. 2. He who seeks, finds, he who asks [1], receives. 3. I will read this book to-day and send it to you to-morrow. 4. My master wants me to play [2] the guitar. 5. Here are two flowers, choose one or the other. 6. Do you know these gentlemen? I do not know them. 7. He wants you to protect [3] the child. 8. When you arrive in New York, send me a letter. 9. I want to pay you but I have no money to-day. 10. Did you find what you were looking for? 11. The laws of the nation protect us. 12. It is not probable that he will conquer [4].

[1] pide. [2] Translate *that I play (pres. subj.)* [3] *Cf.* 4th sentence.
[4] *(pres. subj.)*

CHAPTER XVIII.

REFLEXIVE AND IMPERSONAL VERBS

Reflexive Verbs

166. The reflexive verb is conjugated with an object pronoun representing the same person or thing as the subject. The only reflexive pronoun is the pronoun of the third person: **se** (disjunctive **sí**) which is masculine and feminine, singular and plural, accusative and dative. In the 1st and 2d persons, the conjunctive and disjunctive personal pronouns are regularly used.

The reflexive object pronouns are treated as personal object pronouns (see § **80** to **93**); the subject when a pronoun is expressed or not, according to § **75**.

Ex.—Yo me engaño, me engaño, me engaño yo,	*I deceive myself.*
Él se alaba, se alaba, se alaba él,	*He praises himself.*
Ellos (ellas, V.V.) se alaban, se alaban, etc.	*They praise themselves.*
Quiero disfrazarme,	*I want (wish) to disguise myself.*
disfrazándome . . .	*disguising myself.*
habiéndome disfrazado,	*having disguised myself.*

167. The following tenses may serve as models for the complete conjugation:

Present Indicative	Perfect*
Yo me alabo	me he alabado
tú te alabas	te has alabado
él se alaba	se ha alabado

* *All* reflexive verbs are conjugated with *haber* as auxiliary.

86

Present Indicative	**Perfect**
nosotros nos alabamos	nos hemos alabado
vosotros os alabáis	os habeis alabado
ellos se alaban	se han alabado

168. Every transitive verb may become reflexive as:

Ex.—engañar, *to deceive.* engañarse, *to deceive one's self.*
Me engaña, *he deceives me.* Se engaña, *he deceives himself.*

169. Some verbs have a different meaning when used as reflexives:

Ex.—dormir, *to sleep.* dormirse, *to fall asleep.*
morir, *to die.* morirse, *to be dying.*
ir, *to go.* irse, *to go away.*

170. Many Spanish verbs are used only reflexively; the reflexive form is generally used in preference to the passive.

Ex.—*Always reflexive:*
alegrarse, *to rejoice.*
atreverse á, *to dare to.*
Reflexive for passive:
El periódico se publica . . . *for:* El periódico está publicado . . . } *The paper is published . . .*

171. A reflexive is called reciprocal when the verb refers to two or more persons acting upon one another.

Ex.—Se engañan, *They deceive themselves,* or : *They deceive one another.*

In such cases, **uno** and **otro**, properly inflected, may be added to the verb for emphasis or greater clearness.

Ex.—Se engañan uno á otro, *They deceive one another.*
Se aborrecen una á otra, *They hate one another (fem.)*

Impersonal Verbs

172. Impersonal verbs are inflected according to the conjugation indicated by their infinitive, but they are limited in form to the Infinitive, the Participles and the 3d person singular of other tenses.

Ex.—llover,	*to rain.*
Llueve,	*It rains.*
nevar,	*to snow.*
Nieva,	*It snows.*
Ha llovido mucho,	*It rained a great deal.*
Había nevado,	*It had snowed.*

173. Many transitive verbs are used impersonally while some impersonal verbs assume at times a personal meaning.

Ex.—Basta decir,	*It suffices to say.*
Comienza á llover,	*It begins to rain.*
Amanecí en Sevilla y anochecí en Granada,	*I reached Seville at daybreak, and Granada at nightfall.* (Litt.: *I " dawned " in Seville and " dusked " in Granada.*)

174. In speaking of weather or temperature the verb **hacer**, *to make*, is used impersonally for the English **is**.

| Ex.—Hace buen tiempo, | *It is fine weather.* |
| Hacía mucho calor, | *It was very warm.* |

With expressions of time, **hacer** impersonal means: *it is . . . since, ago.* (See also **haber** § 145.)

| Ex.—Hace quince días que llegué aquí, | *It is fifteen days since I arrived here,* or: *I arrived here fifteen days ago.* |

EXERCISE XVIII.

VOCABULARY XVIII.

llamarse, *to be called.*   levantarse, *to get up, to rise.*

(Also verbs given in preceding Chapter.)

A. 1. Give the Present Indicative, Preterit, and Future Indicative of **alegrarse**, **levantarse**. 2. Mi amigo se llama

Fernando ¿Cómo se llama su amigo de V.? 3. Me he comprado un sombrero nuevo. 4. Este libro se publica en Nueva York. 5. Aquí se habla español. 6. Disfrazándose así, quiere engañarme pero se engaña á sí. 7. Se halla enfermo. 8. Hay que resignarse al destino y tener paciencia. 9. ¿Qué tiempo hace? Hace un frío insoportable. 10. Está nevando hoy, y helará mañana.

B. 1. Did you rise early this morning? I rose at six o'clock. 2. You praise yourselves too much, the glory is not yours. 3. The general did not prepare himself for[1] the battle, and his enemies surprised him. 4. Letters were sent[2] to the soldiers. 5. This house will be sold[3] to-morrow. 6. When they met, they saluted each other courteously. 7. This boy is called Peter. 8. When it rains or snows, the city is more agreeable than the country. 9. What (kind of) weather is[4] it? It is going to[5] rain because it is[4] very windy[6] and hot. 10. In winter night falls[7] very early.

[1] para. [2] Translate as reflexive (subject following verb). [3] Translate as reflexive. [4] Use *hacer*. [5] va á . . . [6] Translate *much wind and heat*. [7] Translate in one word *night falls* (§ **173**).

CHAPTER XIX.

IRREGULAR VERBS

175. A verb is irregular when the stem undergoes changes other than those required to maintain the pronunciation of the Infinitive or to obey the laws of orthography (*cf.* § **160** to **165**).

176. The formation of tenses above given (§ **156**) applies also to most of the irregular verbs, since the irregularities are generally found in the principal parts from which the derived parts are regularly inflected.

177. Verbs which suffer similar variations can be grouped into one class; each class can then be studied by means of a representative verb.

178. Before proceeding with the conjugation of irregular verbs the following remarks should be well understood:

(*a*) All irregular verbs are inflected according to the conjugation to which they belong.

(*b*) Orthographic changes apply to all verbs whether regular or irregular.

(*c*) The Imperfect Indicative is regular in all Spanish verbs except **ir**, *to go* (§ **207**); **ver**, *to see* (§ **220**); **ser**, *to be* (§ **147**).

(*d*) The 2d person plural of the Imperative is *always* regular.

(*e*) Compound verbs are conjugated like their simple verbs unless otherwise stated.

(*f*) All forms not given are regular according to tense-formation explained in § **156**.

IRREGULAR VERBS

1st Class (1st and 2d Conjugation)

179. In this class the stem vowels* e, o become respectively ie, and ue when accented; they resume their original form when the tonic accent falls on another syllable.

Examples:

Stem vowel: E.—1st Conjugation

180. Cerrar, *to shut.* Pres. Part.: **cerrando.** Past Part.: **cerrado.**

Present Indicative:

cierr o†, **cierr** as, **cierr** a, cerr amos, cerr áis, **cierr** an.

Present Subjunctive:

cierr e, **cierr** es, **cierr** e, cerr emos, cerr éis, **cierr** en.

Imperative:

cierr a, cerr ad.

All other tenses regular.

Stem vowel: E.—2d Conjugation

181. Perder, *to lose.* Pres. Part.: **perdiendo.** Past Part.: **perdido.**

Present Indicative:

pierd o, **pierd** es, **pierd** e, perd emos, perd éis, **pierd** en.

Present Subjunctive:

pierd a, **pierd** as, **pierd** a, perd amos, perd áis, **pierd** an.

Imperative:

pierd e, perd ed.

All other tenses regular.

---

* The stem vowel is the one standing nearest to the Infinitive ending.

† Irregular forms in heavy type.

Stem vowel : O.—1st Conjugation *

182. Contar, *to count, to relate.* Pres. Part. : **contando.**
Past Part. : **contado.**

Present Indicative :

cuent o,   cuent as,   cuent a,   cont amos,   cont áis,   cuent an.

Present Subjunctive :

cuent e,   cuent es,   cuent e,   cont emos,   cont éis,   cuent en.

Imperative :

cuent a,   cont ad.

All other tenses regular.

Stem vowel : O.—2d Conjugation

183. Mover, *to move.* Pres. Part. : **moviendo.** Past Part. :
movido.

Present Indicative :

muev o,   muev es,   muev e,   mov emos,   mov éis,   muev en.

Present Subjunctive :

muev a,   muev as,   muev a,   mov amos,   mov áis,   muev an.

Imperative :

muev e,   mov ed.

All other tenses regular.

184. In **errar,** *to err,* the initial i of ie is changed to **y** as
no Spanish word may begin with **ie.**

Errar, *to err.* Pres. Part. : **errando.** Past Part. : **errado.**

Present Indicative :

yerr o,   yerr as,   yerr a,   err amos,   err áis,   yerr an.

Present Subjunctive :

yerr e,   yerr es,   yerr e,   err emos,   err éis,   yerr en.

Imperative :

yerr a,   err ad.

Other tenses without change.

---

*Jugar, to play, belongs also to this class and changes *u* to *ue :*
     Ex.—*jueg o, jueg as,* . . . *jug amos,* etc.

185. In the verb **oler**, *to smell, to scent*, an **h** precedes the **u** of **ue**, as no Spanish word may begin with **ue**.

Oler, *to smell, to scent*. Pres. Part. : **oliendo**. Past Part. : **olido**.

Present Indicative :

huel o,   **huel** es,   **huel** e,   ol emos,   ol éis,   **huel** en.

Present Subjunctive :

huel a,   **huel** as,   **huel** a,   ol amos,   ol áis,   **huel** an.

Imperative :

huel e,   ol ed.

Other tenses without the **h**.

186. Cocer, *to cook, to boil*, belongs to this class of irregular verbs, and does not undergo the orthographic changes indicated in § **163**.

Cocer, *to cook, to boil*. Pres. Part. : **cociendo**. Past Part. : **cocido**.

Present Indicative :

cuez o,   **cuec** es,   **cuec** e,   coc emos,   coc éis,   **cuec** en.

Present Subjunctive :

cuez a,   **cuez** as,   **cuez** a,   coz amos,   coz áis,   **cuez** an.

Imperative :

cuec e,   coc ed.

Other tenses regular.

NOTE.—Verbs belonging to this class, and to the following classes will be found with reference to each class or § in the general list of irregular verbs on page 164. For verbs not given in the lessons, the list should be consulted as several verbs are regular although they appear at first sight to belong to some class of irregular verbs.

EXERCISE XIX.

VOCABULARY XIX.

Model : cerrar

empezar,	*to begin.*
helar,	*to freeze.*
nevar,	*to snow.*
pensar,	*to think.*

Model : contar

acordarse,	*to remember.*
costar,	*to cost.*
mostrar,	*to show.*
volar,	*to fly.*

Model : perder

defender,	*to defend.*
entender,	*to understand.*

Model : mover

llover,	*to rain.*
volver,	*to turn, to return, to come back* (before Infinitive : *to do again*).
vuelto,	*returned* (*irreg.*)

(Also verbs given in the preceding Chapter.)

A. 1. Give : (1) the 3d person singular, Present Indicative of the above verbs. (2) The irregular forms of **pensar, entender, mostrar, volver.** 2. ¿ Por qué no cierra V. la puerta? Hace mucho frío. 3. Un pájaro que vuela se mueve con facilidad en todas direcciones. 4. No hiela ó nieva en Cuba, pero llueve mucho. 5. Este cuarto huele mal, no quiero habitarle. 6. Los muchachos juegan á la pelota esta mañana. 7. No pienso ir á París, cuesta demasiado. 8. Hijo mío, acuérdate de tu promesa, y vuelve pronto. 9. No entiendo lo que me dice.

B. 1. At what hour do you begin to work ? 2. I do not remember at what hour I began this morning. 3. Close [1] the door, we are freezing here. 4. They do not understand each other. 5. Do not believe [1] what he relates ! 6. I wish them to lose [2] no time, notwithstanding what the labor may cost. 7. Come [1] back to-morrow, the judge has not returned yet. 8. Do you think that it will rain [3] this afternoon ? 9. They defend themselves with courage. 10. Bread is baked [4] (cooked) in the oven.

---

[1] Insert *Usted* ; use pres. subj. (§ 147, note). [2] Translate *I wish that they do not lose* . . . [3] (*pres. subj.*) [4] Use reflex. constr. (§ 170).

CHAPTER XX.

2d Class (3d Conjugation)

187. In this class which is composed of verbs of the 3d conjugation, the stem vowels **e** and **o** when accented are expanded to **ie** and **ue** respectively, as is the case in the 1st class. Besides, when unaccented, **e** becomes **i**, and **o** becomes **u**, if the next syllable contains a vowel other than **i**. This takes place in the 1st and 2d persons plural of the Present Subjunctive, the 3d person singular and the 3d plural of the Preterit, in all Subjunctive tenses derived from the Preterit, and in the Present Participle.

Example:

Stem vowel: E

sentir, to feel.

188. Sentir, *to feel.* Pres. Part.: **sint iendo,** Past Part.: **sentido.**

Present Indicative :
sient o, **sient** es, **sient** e, sent imos, sent ís, **sient** en.

Present Subjunctive :
sient a, **sient** as, **sient** a, sint amos, sint áis, **sient** an.

Imperative :
    sient e,   sent id.

Preterit :
sent í, sent iste, **sint** ió, sent imos, sent isteis, **sint** ieron

Imperfect Subjunctive :
sint iera, –ieras, –iera, –iéramos, –ierais, –ieran.

2d Imperfect Subjunctive :

sint iese, –ieses, –iese, –iésemos, –ieseis, –iesen.

Future Subjunctive :

sint iere, –ieres, –iere, –iéremos, –iereis, –ieren.

Future Indicative :	*Present Conditional :*
sentir é (*reg.*)	sentir ía (*reg.*)

Stem vowel: O

dormir, *to sleep.*

189. Dormir, *to sleep.* Pres. Part. : **durm** iendo. Past Part.: **dormido.**

Present Indicative :

duerm o, **duerm** es, **duerm** e, dorm imos, dorm ís, **duerm** en.

Present Subjunctive :

duerm a, **duerm** as, **duerm** a, durm amos, durm áis, **duerm** an.

Imperative :

duerm e,   dorm id.

Preterit :

dorm í, dorm iste, **durm** ió, dorm imos, dorm isteis, **durm** ieron.

Imperfect Subjunctive :

durm iera, –ieras, –iera, –iéramos, –ierais, –ieran.

2d Imperfect Subjunctive :

durm iese, –ieses, –iese, –iésemos, –ieseis, –iesen.

Future Subjunctive :

durm iere, –ieres, –iere, –iéremos, –iereis, –ieren.

Future Indicative :	*Present Conditional :*
dormir é (*reg.*)	dormir ía (*reg.*)

190. Adquirir, *to acquire ;* **discernir,** *to discern,* are conjugated like verbs of the first class, **i** and **e** becoming **ie** when accented.

Irregular Verbs.—3d Class (3d Conjugation)

191. This class is composed only of verbs of the 3d conjugation with the stem vowel **e**. The stem vowel **e** becomes **i** when accented, and also when unaccented if the following syllable contains a vowel other than **i**, the latter change taking place in the same forms as those indicated in the preceding class.

Examples:

192. Servir, *to serve.* Pres. Part.: **sirv** iendo. Past Part.: servido.

Present Indicative:

sirv o, sirv es, sirv e, serv imos, serv ís, **sirv en.**

Present Subjunctive:

sirv a, sirv as, sirv a, sirv amos, sirv áis, **sirv an.**

Imperative:

sirv e, serv id,

Preterit:

serv í, serv iste, sirv ió, serv imos, serv isteis, sirv ieron.

Imperfect Subjunctive:

sirv iera, –ieras, –iera, –iéramos, –ierais, –ieran.

2d Imperfect Subjunctive:

sirv iese, –ieses, –iese, –iésemos, –ieseis, –iesen.

Future Subjunctive:

sirv iere, –ieres, –iere, –iéremos, –iereis, –ieren.

Future Indicative: *Present Conditional:*
servir é (*reg.*) servir ía (*reg.*)

193. Verbs ending in **eir,** on changing the stem vowel **e** to **i** lose the **i** of terminations beginning with **ie** and **io.**

Examples:

Reir, *to laugh.* Pres. Part.: **riendo** (not. riiendo). Past Part.: **reido.**

Preterit :

re í,   re íste,   **ri** ó,   re ímos,   re ísteis,   **ri** eron

Imperfect Subjunctive :   *2d Imperfect Subjunctive :*
  ri era (not ri iera).   **ri** ese.

Future Subjunctive :   *Future Indicative :*
  ri ere.   reir é.

Present Conditional :
  reir ía.

Irregular Verbs.—4th Class (3d Conjugation)

194. This class is composed of verbs ending in **uir, üir,** in which the **u** is pronounced (not those in –**guir** or –**quir**). When accented or followed by **a** or **o,** the **u** becomes **uy.** The **i** of terminations beginning with **ie** or **io** changes to **y** when unaccented since it comes between two vowels, according to § **164.**

Examples :

195. Instruir, *to instruct.* Pres. Part.: **instruyendo.** Past Part.: **instruido.**

Present Indicative :
instruy o, **instruy** es, **instruy** e, instru imos,   instru ís,
          instruy en.

Present Subjunctive :
instruy a, **instruy** as, **instruy** a, **instruy** amos, **instruy** áis,
          instruy an.

Imperative :
    instruy e   instru id.

Preterit :
instru í,   instru iste, instru **y**ó, instru imos,   instru isteis,
          instru **y**eron.

Imperfect Subjunctive :
instru **y**era,   –**y**eras,   –**y**era,   –**y**éramos,   –**y**erais,   –**y**eran.

2d Imperfect Subjunctive:

instru **y**ese, –**y**eses, –**y**ese, –**y**ésemos, –**y**eseis, –**y**esen.

Future Subjunctive:

instru **y**ere, –**y**eres, –**y**ere, –**y**éremos, –**y**ereis, –**y**eren.

Future Indicative:	*Present Conditional:*
instruir é.	instruir ía.

NOTE.—*Imperfect Indicative:* **instruía**, etc., accented **i** between two vowels.

EXERCISE XX.

VOCABULARY XX.

Model: sentir

arrepentirse,	*to repent.*
concernir,	*to concern.*
herir,	*to wound.*
preferir,	*to prefer.*

Model: dormir

morir,   *to die.* (Past Part. *muerto,* see Chapter XXIII.)

Model: servir

pedir,	*to ask* *.
rendir,	*to render* †.
reñir,	*to quarrel, to scold.*
seguir,	*to follow, to keep on.*

Model: instruir

destruir,	*to destroy.*
distribuir,	*to distribute.*
huir,	*to flee.*

(Also verbs given in the preceding Chapter.)

A. 1. Give the 3d person singular of the Present Indicative and the 3d person plural of the Preterit of the above verbs. 2. Conjugate : **preferir, pedir**. 3. Siento dejar á París, pero vuelvo á los Estados Unidos. 4. Pidió licencia para ir á su tierra pero se la negó el amo. 5. Prefirieron el empleo de soldado al de comerciante y se arrepienten ahora.

---

* *Pedir* is : To ask for something. *Preguntar* is : To ask solely for information.

† *Rendirse,* To surrender.

6. ¿Cómo se siente su hermana de V.? Está un poco mejor.
7. Siguió su camino sin atreverse á mirar hacia atrás, como
si hubiese hecho (*done*) algo malo.   8. Muriendo por la
patria, se muere con gloria.   9. Este abogado instruye á su
hijo en las leyes del estado.   10. El filósofo se ríe de las
locuras de los hombres.

B. 1. These two men are quarrelling[1], but it is an affair
that does not concern me.   2. Our enemies did not flee and
did not surrender, because they preferred (the[2]) death to
(the[2]) captivity.   3. This poor man[3] does not ask anything,
but I prefer to[3] give him a little (of[5]) money because he
needs it.   4. He wounded two of his adversaries although
he himself[4] had been wounded.   5. They loved them in
spite of all, but their affection served only to cause (to[5])
them new sorrows.   6. The Spaniards sleep an hour after
(the[2]) dinner.   7. The enemies destroyed the walls of the
city and the commander of the place surrendered.   8. This
boy always asks for[6] money; his father scolds him, but he
keeps on asking.   9. The charitable persons distribute food
to the poor[7].   10. The study of (the[2]) languages demands[8]
the greatest application.

[1] (*reflexive*).   [2] Insert article in Spanish.   [3] Omit.   [4] mismo.   [5] Insert.
[6] Omit.   [7] (*plural*).   [8] pedir.

CHAPTER XXI.

IRREGULAR VERBS——Continued

196. Some irregular verbs, although most commonly used, cannot easily be divided into classes. Their inflection should be learned separately and carefully.

197. Andar, *to go*;* **andando, andado.**

Present Indicative†: (reg.)

and o,   and as,   and a,   and amos,   and áis,   and an

Preterit:

anduv e,   **anduv** iste,   **anduv** o,   –imos,   –isteis,   –ieron.

Imperfect Subjunctive:

anduv iera,   –ieras,   –iera,   –iéramos,   –ierais,   –ieran.

2d Imperfect Subjunctive:

anduv iese,   –ieses,   –iese,   –iésemos,   –ieseis,   –iesen.

Future Subjunctive:

anduv iere,   –ieres,   –iere,   –iéremos,   –iereis,   –ieren.

198. Caber, *to be contained in, to fit;* **cabiendo, cabido.**

Present Indicative:

quep o,   cab es,   cab e,   cab emos,   cab éis,   cab en.

Present Subjunctive:

quep a,   **quep** as,   **quep** a,   **quep** amos,   **quep** áis,   **quep** an.

---

* *Andar* means: to go, in a general sense; to go to a definite place or with a purpose is: *ir* § 207.

† Derived parts where not given are regularly formed according to § 156. (Irregular forms in heavy type.)

Preterit:

cup e,   **cup** iste, **cup** o,   **cup** imos,   **cup** isteis, **cup** ieron.

Imperfect Subjunctive:

cup iera, –ieras,   –iera,   –iéramos,   –ierais,   –ieran.

2d Imperfect Subjunctive:

cup iese, –ieses,   –iese,   –iésemos,   –ieseis,   –iesen.

Future Subjunctive:

cup iere, –ieres,   –iere,   –iéremos,   –iereis,   –ieren.

Future Indicative:

cabr é,   –ás,   –á,   –emos,   –éis,   –an.

Present Conditional:

cabr ía,   –ías,   –ía,   –íamos,   –íais,   –íɛn.

Imperative:	*Imperfect Indicative:*
cab e, cab ed.	cab ía, etc.

199. Caer, *to fall;* **cayendo, caído.**

Present Indicative:

caig o,   ca es,   ca e,   ca emos,   ca éis,   ca en.

Present Subjunctive:

caig a, **caig** as, **caig** a, **caig** amos, **caig** áis, **caig** an.

Imperative:

       ca e,   ca ed.

Preterit:

ca í,   ca iste, ca yó, ca ímos,   ca ísteis, ca yeron.

Imperfect Subjunctive:	*2d Imperfect Subjunctive:*
ca yera.	ca yese.
Future Subjunctive:	*Imperfect Indicative:*
ca yere.	ca ía.
Future:	*Present Conditional:*
caer é.	caer ía.

200. Dar, *to give;* **dando, dado.**

Present Indicative :

doy,　　d as,　　d a,　　d amos,　　d ais,　　d an.

Present Subjunctive :

d é,　　d es,　　d é,　　d emos,　　d eis,　　d en.

Imperative :

d a,　　　　　　d ad.

Preterit :

d í,　　d iste,　　d ió,　　d imos,　　d isteis,　　d ieron.

Imperfect Subjunctive :	*2d Imperfect Subjunctive :*
d iera.	d iese.
Future Subjunctive :	*Imperfect Indicative .*
d iere.	d aba.
Future Indicative :	*Present Conditional :*
dar é.	dar ía.

201. Decir, *to say, to tell;* **diciendo, dicho.**

Present Indicative :

dig o,　　dic es,　　dic e,　　dec imos,　　dec ís,　　dic en.

Present Subjunctive :

dig a,　　dig as,　　dig a,　　dig amos,　　dig áis,　　dig an.

Imperative :

dí,　　　　　　dec id.

Preterit :

dije　　dij iste,　　dijo,　　dij imos,　　dij isteis,　　dij eron.

Imperfect Subjunctive :

dij era,　　−eras,　　−era,　　−éramos,　　−erais,　　−eran.

2d Imperfect Subjunctive :

dij ese,　　−eses,　　−ese,　　−ésemos,　　−eseis,　　−esen.

Future Subjunctive :

dij ere,　　−eres,　　−ere,　　−éremos,　　−ereis,　　−eren.

Future Indicative:

dir é,   –ás,   –á,   –emos,   –éis,   –án.

Present Conditional:

dir ía,   –ías,   –ía,   –íamos,   –íais,   –ían.

Imperfect Indicative:

decía.

202. The compounds of **decir** are conjugated like **decir**, except that they have in the 2d person singular of the Imperative –**dice** instead of –**dí**.

Bendecir*, *to bless;* **maldecir**, *to curse,* are regular in the Future and Conditional: **bendeciré, maldeciría.**

203. Ducir, *to lead,* is to be found only in compounds, of which the following will serve as an example.

Conducir, *to conduct, to lead;* **conduciendo, conducido.**

Present Indicative:

conduzc o, conduc es, conduc e, conduc imos, conduc ís, conduc en.

Present Subjunctive:

conduzc a, –duzc as, –duzc a,   –duzc amos, –duzc áis, –duzc an.

Imperative:

conduc e,   conduc id.

Preterit:

conduje,   conduj iste, condujo,   conduj imos, conduj isteis, conduj eron.

Imperfect Subjunctive:	*2d Imperfect Subjunctive:*
conduj era, etc.	conduj ese, etc.
Future Subjunctive:	*Future Indicative:*
conduj ere, etc.	conducir é.
Present Conditional:	*Imperfect Indicative:*
conducir ía.	conduc ía.

* For irregularities in Past Participles see § **224.**

204. Estar, *to be.* See conjugation, § **150.**

205. Haber, *to have* (aux.). See conjugation, § **142.**

206. Hacer, *to do, to make ;* **haciendo, hecho.**

Present Indicative :

hag o,   hac es,   hac e,   hac emos,   hac éis,   hac en.

Present Subjunctive :

hag a,   **hag** as,   **hag** a,   **hag** amos,   **hag** áis,   **hag** an.

Imperative :

haz,   hac ed.

Preterit :

hice,   **hic** iste,   **hizo,**   **hic** imos,   **hic** isteis,   **hic** ieron.

Imperfect Subjunctive :   *2d Imperfect Subjunctive :*
    hic iera.   **hic** iese.

Future Subjunctive :
    hic iere.

Future Indicative :

har é,   –ás,   –á,   –emos,   –éis,   –án.

Present Conditional :

har ía,   –ías,   –ía,   –íamos,   –íais,   –ían.

Imperfect Indicative :
    hac ía, etc.

NOTE.—Compounds of **hacer** conjugated as above, except **satisfacer** which retains the original Latin *f* throughout the conjugation, and has two forms in the 2d person singular of Imperative : **satisfaz, satisface.**

207. Ir, *to go* (see **andar,** § **197,** note); **yendo, ido.**

Present Indicative :

voy,   **vas,**   **va,**   **vamos,**   **vais,**   **van.**

Present Subjunctive :

vay a,   **vəy** as,   **vay** a,   **vay** amos,   **vay** áis,   **vay** an.

Imperative :

    ve,   **vamos** [1],   **id.**

[1] Instead of *vayamos.*

Preterit :

fu í [1],   fu iste,   **fué**,   fu imos,   fu isteis,   **fu eron**.

Imperfect Subjunctive :   *2d Imperfect Subjunctive :*
        fu era [1].   fu ese [1].

Future Subjunctive :   *Future Indicative :*
        fu ere [1].   ir é, etc. (*reg.*)

Present Conditional :
        ir ía, etc. (*reg.*)

Imperfect Indicative :

iba,   ibas,   iba,   íbamos,   ibais,   iban.

208. Oír, *to hear ;* **oyendo, oído.**

Present Indicative :

oig o,   oy es,   oy e,   o ímos,   o ís,   oy en.

Present Subjunctive :

oig a,   oig as,   oig a,   oig amos,   oig áis,   oig an.

Imperative :
        oy e,   o íd.

Preterit :

o í,   o íste,   o yó,   o ímos,   o ísteis,   o yeron.

Imperfect Subjunctive :   *2d Imperfect Subjunctive :*
        o yera, etc.   o yese.

Future Subjunctive :   *Future Indicative :*
        o yere.   oir é.

Present Conditional :   *Imperfect Indicative :*
        oir ía.   o ía.

EXERCISE XXI.

VOCABULARY XXI.

(Verbs given in preceding Chapter.)

A. 1. Andaré, anduve, anda, anduvo. 2. Quepo, cupo, ca-
bré, cupe, cabe. 3. Cae, cayó, caiga*, caigo, caen. 4. Doy,

[1] Same as that of *ser,* § 147.

* When one verb form is the same for two persons, give both persons.
Ex. : *caiga,* 1st pers. sing., 3d pers. sing., Present Subjunctive of *caer.*

da, dé, dí, dió. 5. Dijo, dice, digo, dijimos, digan. 6. Conduce, conduzca, conduje, condujera. 7. Haga, hago, hizo, hice, hará, hace. 8. Va, vaya, iré, vamos, iba, irá. 9. Oigo, oí, oyeron, oye, oía. 10. Me dieron algunos libros que mi hermano les dió el otro día. 11. ¿Por qué anda V. tan de prisa? 12. Por todas partes, sólo se oían los gritos de los que peleaban, y los gemidos de los que caían; no se veía otra cosa que muertos, heridos y sangre; cayeron más de dos mil hombres . . . 13. En este cuarto no cabrán trescientas personas. 14. Díme con quien andas y te diré quien eres. 15. Este hombre me ha hecho perder toda la mañana. 16. Permita V. que le conduzca á la casa del juez. 17. Me voy de Madrid. 18. No digas nunca: "Haré esto mañana." Lo que está hecho vale *(is worth,* § **215**) más que lo que se ha de hacer.

B. 1. An old proverb says that misers never do good[1] except[2] when they die. 2. Where were you going when I met you? 3. To-morrow I shall go to see some friends of[3] mine who prefer to live in the country. 4. My neighbor gave (to) his son a gold watch four months ago[4]. It[3] does not go well because it[3] fell from his pocket. 5. Patience and reflexion make easy many things which appeared impossible at first sight. 6. What will you do on[5] Wednesday afternoon[6]? I will go to the opera. 7. Did you hear what this man said[7]? I heard him say that he[3] fell down[3] in the street. 8. Let us go to the theater. 9. I read and translate two or three pages of Spanish every day. 10. This box holds all my books[8].

---

[1] bien.   [2] sino.   [3] Omit.   [4] See § **174.**   [5] el.   [6] por la tarde.   [7] **Translate** *what said this man.*   [8] See sentence 13 under *A.*

CHAPTER XXII.

IRREGULAR VERBS——Concluded

209. Poder, *to be able ;* **pudiendo, podido.**

Present Indicative :

pued o, **pued** es, **pued** e, pod emos, pod éis, **pued** en.

Present Subjunctive :

pued a, **pued** as, **pued** a, pod amos, pod áis, **pued** an.

Preterit :

pude, **pud** iste, **pudo,** **pud** imos, **pud** isteis, **pud** ieron.

Imperfect Subjunctive :   *2d Imperfect Subjunctive :*
    pud iera, etc.   **pud**iese, etc.

Future Subjunctive :
pud iere, etc.

Future Indicative :

podr é, –ás, –á, –emos, –éis, –án.

Present Conditional :

podr ía, –ías, –ía, –íamos, –íais, –ían.

Imperfect Indicative :   *Imperative :*
    pod ía, etc.   Wanting.

210. Poner, *to put, to place ;* **poniendo, puesto.**

Present Indicative :

pong o, pon es, pon e, pon emos, pon éis, pon en.

Present Subjunctive :

pong a, **pong** as, **pong** a, **pong** amos, **pong** áis, **pong** an.

Imperative :

pon,   pon ed.

Preterit :

puse,   pus iste,   puso,   pus imos,   pus isteis,   pus ieron.

Imperfect Subjunctive :   *2d Imperfect Subjunctive :*
   pus iera, etc.   pus iese.

Future Subjunctive :
     pus iere.

Future Indicative :

pondr é,   –ás,   –á,   –emos,   –éis,   –án.

Present Conditional :

pondr ía,   –ías,   –ía,   –íamos,   –íais,   –ían.

Imperfect Indicative :
     pon ía, etc.

211. Querer, *to want, to wish ;* **queriendo, querido.**

Present Indicative :

quier o,   quier es,   quier e,   quer emos,   quer éis,   quier en.

Present Subjunctive :

quier a,   quier as,   quier a,   quer amos,   quer áis,   quier an.

Imperative :
     quier e,   quer ed.

Preterit :

quise,   quis iste,   quiso,   quis imos,   quis isteis,   quis ieron.

Imperfect Subjunctive :   *2d Imperfect Subjunctive :*
   quis iera, etc.   quis iese.

Future Subjunctive :
     quis iere.

Future Indicative :

querr é,   –ás,   –á,   –emos,   –éis,   –án.

Present Conditional :

querr ía,   –ías,   –ía,   –íamos,   –íais,   –ían.

Imperfect Indicative :
     quer ía, etc.

212. Saber, *to know*[1], *to know how;* **sabiendo, sabido.**

Present Indicative:

sé,   sab es,   sab e,   sab emos,   sab éis,   sab en.

Present Subjunctive:

sep a,   **sep** as,   **sep** a,   **sep** amos,   **sep** áis,   **sep** an.

Imperative:

sab e,   sab ed.

Preterit:

supe,   sup iste,   **supo,   sup** imos,   **sup** isteis,   **sup** ieron.

Imperfect Subjunctive: *2d Imperfect Subjunctive:*
    sup iera, etc.   **sup** iese.

Future Subjunctive:
    sup iere.

Future Indicative:

sabr é,   –ás,   –á,   –emos,   –éis,   –án.

Present Conditional:

sabr ía,   –ías,   –ía,   –íamos,   –íais,   –ían.

Imperfect Indicative:
    sab ía, etc.

213. Ser, *to be.*   See conjugation, § 147.

214. Salir, *to go out, to come out;* **saliendo, salido.**

Present Indicative:

salg o,   sal es,   sal e,   sal imos,   sal ís,   sal en.

Present Subjunctive:

salg a,   **salg** as,   **salg** a,   **salg** amos,   **salg** áis,   **salg** an.

Imperative:

sal,   sal id.

Preterit:

sal í,   sal iste,   sal ió,   sal imos,   sal isteis,   sal ieron.

Imperfect Subjunctive: *2d Imperfect Subjunctive:*
    sal iera, etc.   sal iese, etc.

Future Subjunctive:
    sal iere.

[1] *Saber,* to know, in speaking of things; to know, meaning *to be acquainted,* is in Spanish: *conocer.*   **§ 163.**

Future Indicative :

saldr é,　　–ás,　　　–á,　　　–emos,　　　–éis,　　　–án.

Present Conditional:

saldr ía,　　–ías,　　　–ía,　　　–íamos,　　　–íais,　　　–ían.

Imperfect Indicative :

sal ía, etc.

215. Valer, *to be worth,* is conjugated exactly like **salir,** changing **s** to **v,** except in Present Indicative, 2d plural, **val éis** for **val ís** (**valer** being 2d conjugation), and that it has the regular Imperative, 2d singular, **vale** besides **val.** The 2d person plural is of course **valed,** (*Cf.* § **178, d**).

216. Tener, *to have, to possess* (see § **142**); **teniendo, tenido.**

Present Indicative :

teng o,　　**tien** es,　　**tien** e,　　ten emos,　　ten éis,　　**tien** en.

Present Subjunctive :

teng a,　　**teng** as,　　**teng** a,　　**teng** amos,　　**teng** áis,　　**teng** an.

Imperative :

ten,　　　　　　　　　　ten ed.

Preterit :

tuve,　　**tuv** iste,　**tuvo,**　　**tuv** imos,　　**tuv** isteis,　**tuv** ieron.

Imperfect Subjunctive :　　　　　　　*2d Imperfect Subjunctive :*

　tuv iera, etc.　　　　　　　　　　　**tuv** iese, etc.

Future Subjunctive :

tuv iere.

Future Indicative :

tendr é,　　–ás,　　　–á,　　　–emos,　　　–éis,　　　–án.

Present Conditional :

tendr ía,　　–ías,　　　–ía,　　　–íamos,　　　–íais,　　　–ían.

Imperfect Indicative :

ten ía, etc.

217. Traer, *to bring;* **trayendo, traído.**

Present Indicative:

traig o,   tra es,   tra e,   tra emos,   tra éis.   tra en.

Present Subjunctive:

traig a,   **traig** as,   **traig** a,   **traig** amos,   **traig** áis,   **traig** an.

Imperative:

tra e,   tra ed.

Preterit:

traje,   **traj** iste,   **trajo,**   **traj** imos,   **traj** isteis, **traj** eron.

Imperfect Subjunctive: *Future Indicative:*

traj era, etc.   traer é, etc.

2d Imperfect Subjunctive: *Present Conditional:*

traj ese, etc.   traer ía, etc.

Future Subjunctive: *Imperfect Indicative:*

traj ere, etc.   tra ía, etc.

218. Valer, *to be worth.* See **salir,** § 214.

219. Venir, *to come;* **viniendo, venido.**

Present Indicative:

veng o,   **vien** es,   **vien** e,   ven imos,   ven ís,   **vien** en.

Present Subjunctive:

veng a,   **veng** as,   **veng** a,   **veng** amos,   **veng** áis,   **veng** an.

Imperative:

ven,   ven id.

Preterit:

vine,   **vin** iste,   **vino,**   **vin** imos,   **vin** isteis,   **vin** ieron.

Imperfect Subjunctive: *2d Imperfect Subjunctive:*

vin iera, etc.   **vin** iese, etc.

Future Subjunctive:

vin iere.

Future Indicative:

vendr é,   –ás,   –á,   –emos,   –éis,   –án.

Present Conditional:

vendr ía,   –ías,   –ía,   –íamos,   –íais,   –ían.

Imperfect Indicative:

ven ía,   ven ías, etc.

220. Ver, *to see ;* **viendo, visto.**

Present Indicative :

ve o,   v es,   v e,   v emos,   v eis,   v en.

Present Subjunctive :

ve a,   **ve** as,   **ve** a,   **ve** amos,   **ve** áis,   **ve** an.

Imperative :

v e,   v ed.

Preterit :

v í,   v iste,   v ió,   v imos,   v isteis,   v ieron.

Imperfect Subjunctive :   *2d Imperfect Subjunctive :*
   v iera, etc.   v iese, etc.

Future Subjunctive :   *Future Indicative :*
   v iere, etc.   ver é,   ver ás.

Present Conditional :

ver ía,   ver ías, etc.

Imperfect Indicative :

ve ía,   **ve** ías,   **ve** ía,   **ve** íamos,   **ve** íais,   **ve** ían.

EXERCISE XXII.

VOCABULARY XXII.

Ponerse,   *to become, to set.*   (See *A.* 17.)

(Also verbs given in preceding Chapter.)

A. 1. Puedo, podrá, podemos, pudimos, pudo, podría*.
2. Puso, pongo, puse, pondrán, pone. 3. Quieren, quise,
querré, querían, querrían, quiera. 4. Sé, sabrá, supe, saben,
sepa. 5. Sale, salgamos, saldrá, salen, salieron. 6. Valió,
valdrán, vale, valga. 7. Tenga, tuve, tendré, tuvieron, tenemos. 8. Traigo, traen, traiga, trajimos, traerán. 9. Venga,
vienen, vendremos, vengo, vinieron. 10. Veo, ven, vean,

---

* See foot-note to Exercise XXI.

vió, veíamos, vieron.   11. Cuando no podemos lograr lo que deseamos debemos contentarnos con lo que tenemos. 12. Fuimos á ver el convento, y la mejor cosa que vimos fué la librería.   13. Pedro vino á las diez, y salió á las once. 14. Más vale una injuria que una lisonja.   15. Si al salir de tu casa vieres volar cuervos, déjalos volar, y mira tú donde pones los pies (Quevedo).   16. Traiga V. las flores que compré ayer.   17. Se pone el sol á las cinco, y sale la luna á las seis.   18. Véngase V. esta tarde y podremos ir al concierto. 19. No se sabe si el invierno será frío.   20. Este comerciante se ha puesto rico en poco tiempo.

B. 1. You are reading the paper; what news does it[1] contain[2]?   2. The general did not wish to pursue the[3] enemy for fear of an ambuscade.   3. It is clear that he who does not pay either[4] cannot or will not pay[1].   4. I know the judge; he will do for[5] you all that[6] he can[7].   5. We have come out of the house to take the air in the garden, where it is[8] cooler than in the room.   6. When he heard my answer, he became furious.   7. Honor is worth more than money[9]. 8. Let us see what he says in his letter.   9. He can do nothing and lives on[10] what his neighbors bring (to) him. 10. My father came to this country when he was[11] twenty years old[1].   11. Can you lend me ten dollars? I should do it with much pleasure if I had[12] it[13] with me.   12. Who knows?

[1] Omit.   [2] Translate *brings*.   [3] al.   [4] Translate (*it*) *is because*.   [5] para. [6] cuanto.   [7] Pres. Subj.   [8] Use *hacer*.   [9] See sentence 14 under *A*.   [10] de. [11] Translate *had*.   [12] Imp. Subj.   [13] Translate *them*.

CHAPTER XXIII.

IRREGULAR PAST PARTICIPLES.—ORDER OF WORDS.—
INTERROGATIVE SENTENCES.—PERSONAL ACCUSATIVE

Irregular Past Participle

221. A past participle which does not end in **–ado**, or **–ido**
like those of the model verbs is said to be irregular.

222. The following verbs, otherwise regular, have an irregular past participle:

abrir,	*to open.*	abierto,	*opened.*
cubrir,	*to cover.*	cubierto,	*covered.*
escribir,	*to write.*	escrito,	*written.*
imprimir,	*to print.*	impreso,	*printed.*

NOTE.—The compounds of the first three have the same
irregularity in the past participle as the simple verbs.

Ex.—descubrir, *to discover.* descubierto, *discovered.*

223. The following irregular verbs and their compounds
have an irregular past participle:

morir (2d class), *to die.*	muerto, *dead, killed.* (See § **228**.)
solver (1st class), *to loosen.*	suelto, *loosened.*
volver " *to turn, to return.*	vuelto, *turned, returned.*

(Other irregular past participles have been given in preceding Chapters, with the conjugation of their respective verbs.)

224. Contradecir, *to contradict;* **bendecir,** *to bless,* and **maldecir,** *to curse,* have the regular past participle in **–ido**, not in **–dicho** like **decir.** The last two have also the irregular forms **bendito, maldito,** now used only as adjectives.

225. A number of verbs have two past participles: one
regular, the other irregular. The first usually refers to an

action and is used with **haber** in the active, or **ser** in the passive, voice; the second indicates a state or the result of the action and follows **estar**, becoming practically an adjective.

Ex.—Hemos despertado temprano, *We woke up early.*

Estamos despiertos, *We are awake.*

Después de haber sepultado á muchos muertos, encontraron otros cadáveres insepultos, *After having buried many dead, they found other bodies unburied.*

El abogado le ha confundido, y el pobre hombre está muy confuso, *The lawyer has confused him, and the poor man is very much confused.*

226. Prender, *to take*, has the two participles **prendido** and **preso**, which are interchangeable in the sense of: *to arrest;* otherwise the above distinction holds good.

Ex.—Han prendido (*or* preso) dos ladrones, *They have arrested two robbers.*

El reo ha sido preso, *The culprit has been arrested.*

El fuego ha prendido en la casa, *Fire has broken out in the house (the house has taken fire).*

NOTE.—Compounds of **prender** form their past participle regularly.

227. Romper, *to break*, has the two participles: **rompido** and **roto**. The first form is used when the verb is intransitive; the second in all other cases.

Ex.—Ha rompido con su amigo, *He has broken with his friend.*

El viento ha roto muchos árboles, *The wind has broken many trees.*

El vaso está roto, *The vase is broken.*

NOTE.—Compounds of **romper** form their past participles regularly.

228. **Muerto** is used instead of **matado,** *killed,* when applied to persons. Referring to animals, as a reflexive, or in the figurative sense, **matado** is regularly employed.

Ex.—Un ladrón le ha muerto,	*A robber has killed him.*
El capitán fué muerto por sus soldados,	*The captain was killed by his soldiers.*
Han matado tres vacas,	*They have killed three cows.*
Se ha matado *,	*He has killed himself.*
Me ha matado con su charlería,	*He has worn me out with his gossip.*

Order of Words

229. In Spanish, much more freedom is allowed in arranging the words of a sentence than in English. Provided the clearness is not diminished, the order of words is left almost entirely to the writer's idea of elegance or harmony.

Ex.—La llegada del viajero causó una gran alegría á todos sus amigos.

Causó la llegada del viajero una gran alegría á todos sus amigos.

A todos sus amigos, causó una gran alegría la llegada del viajero.

Una gran alegría causó la llegada del viajero á todos sus amigos.

The arrival of the traveler gave (caused) great joy to all his friends.

230. Care should be taken however not to separate words belonging naturally together, as a noun from the article or adjective, a relative from its antecedent, etc.

* *Se ha muerto* would mean : he has died (from *morirse*).

Interrogative Sentences

231. In interrogative sentences, the subject, when expressed is placed after the verb; in compound tenses the subject follows the past participle *.

Ex.—¿ Vendrá V. ?　　　　　*Will you come ?*

¿ Tiene él coches y caballos ?　　*Has he carriages and horses ?*

¿ Nos lo dirá V. ?　　　　*Will you tell it to us ?*

¿ Qué dicen ?　　　　　　*What do they say ?*

¿ Qué busca el niño ?　　　*What is the child looking for ?*

¿ He dicho yo tal cosa ?　　*Have I said (did I say) such thing ?*

¿ Han llegado sus amigos de V. ?　*Have your friends arrived ?*

Note.—Interrogative and negative sentences in Spanish are formed without the help of any auxiliary corresponding to the English *do* or *did*.

232. When the subject is a noun, it usually follows the object in interrogations. However, if the object is longer than the subject, it preferably comes last.

Ex.—¿ Quieren juguetes los hijos de V. ?　*Do your children want toys ?*

¿ Fueron al campo los soldados ?　*Did the soldiers go to the camp ?*

¿ Ha leído el muchacho la historia de los Estados Unidos ?　*Has the boy read the history of the United States ?*

233. As an interrogative sentence could not always be distinguished from an affirmative, by its form or by the position of the subject, an inverted question mark (¿) is placed before the sentence in addition to the usual question

---

* *Nosotros* and *vosotros* are sometimes found between the auxiliary forms *hemos*, *habeis*, and the past participle.

mark after it. The same remark applies to exclamative sentences.

Ex.—Tiene buenas casas el vecino de V.　*Your neighbor has good houses.*

　¿Tiene buenas casas el vecino de V.?　*Has your neighbor good houses?*

　¡Qué bien habla!　*How well he speaks!*

Personal Accusative

234. An important difference between Spanish and English is the use of the preposition **á** before a direct object. This preposition is only a grammatical device, and should not be translated.

Ex.—Pedro ama **á** sus padres,　*Peter loves his parents.*
　El reo teme **al** juez,　*The culprit fears the judge.*

235. The principal cases in which **á** is used are the following:

1. Before a noun representing a definite person or a personified thing.

Ex.—Leo **á** Cervántes,　*I read Cervantes.*
　La madre llama **á** su hijo,　*The mother calls her son.*
　No halló **á** ninguno de sus amigos,　*He did not find any of his friends.*
　El soldado defiende **á** su patria,　*The soldier defends his country.*

2. Before proper names of things, unless the definite article is a part of the name.

Ex.—Deseo ver **á** Toledo,　*I wish to see Toledo.*
　Los Moros conquistaron **á** España,　*The Moors conquered Spain.*
　Visitaré la Coruña,　*I shall visit Corunna.*

236. **Á** should not be used :

1. Before common nouns representing things.

Ex.—Perdí mi sombrero,   *I lost my hat.*
No tiene dinero,   *He has no money.*

2. Before nouns representing persons, when taken in an indefinite sense.

Ex.—El comerciante busca un   *The merchant is looking for a*
criado,   *servant.*
but : Busco **á** mi criado,   *I am looking for my servant.*
Hallará amigos en la   *He will find friends in the city.*
ciudad,
but : Halló **á** sus amigos en   *He found his friends in the parlor.*
la sala,
Admitió tres oficiales,   *He admitted three officers.*

3. Before nouns denoting persons, when a true preposition is required to indicate the dative.

Ex.—Envió su criado á la   *He sent his servant to the store.*
tienda,
Presenta su hijo al ge-   *He presents his son to the general.*
neral,
Me presenta el hermano   *He presents to me the brother of his*
de su amigo,   *friend.*
Cf. : Me presenta **al** hermano   *He presents me to the brother of his*
de su amigo,   *friend.*

237. **Á** is also used to distinguish the direct object from the subject when both are nouns representing things; otherwise ambiguity might result from the freedom of construction.

Ex.—El verano sigue á la
primavera,
Á la primavera sigue el   *Summer follows spring.*
verano,
No alcanzó la liebre á   *The hare did not overtake the turtle.*
la tortuga,

238. When applied to persons, certain verbs modify their meaning if they are constraed with **á**. Note the following:

Pierde su amigo,	*He loses his friend.*
Perdió á su amigo,	*He caused the ruin of his friend.*
querer un maestro,	*to want a teacher.*
querer á un maestro,	*to love a teacher.*
Los gitanos roban los niños,	*The gypsies steal children.*
Los gitanos roban á los niños,	*The gypsies rob the children.*

EXERCISE XXIII.

VOCABULARY XXIII.

(For new words in this, and the following Exercises, see General Vocabulary at the end of the book.)

A. 1. En el invierno la tierra está cubierta con un espeso manto de nieve. 2. De los ladrones han muerto á tres y han preso los demás. 3. He leído todos los libros que este autor ha escrito. 4. Aquí tiene el río una anchura de media milla. 5. ¿Qué dice el padre á su hijo? Le dice que va á salir para la ciudad. 6. ¿Quieren los muchachos leer la historia de su patria? 7. ¿Ha recibido el soldado las órdenes del oficial? 8. ¿Lo entiende V. ó no lo entiende? 9. No hallaron allí á ninguno de los huéspedes. 10. El verano que da vida á los campos, mata á las ciudades.

B. 1. Has the captain returned from the war? No, he was killed in the first battle. 2. The storm has broken many panes of glass in our country house. 3. It is very cold here because the windows are open. 4. I have not seen the book, but I believe that it is well written and well printed. 5. Does your friend live in the country or in the city? 6. Have you given to the servant the letters which I wrote yesterday? 7. He entered[1] the parlor and saluted the ladies who were there. 8. The steamer did not overtake the sail boat. 9. The general called the officers to a conference. 10. With two hundred of his soldiers he routed five hundred of the enemy[2]. 11. He is a soldier who honors his country. 12. The Greeks conquered Troy after a siege of ten years. 13. He recommended his servant to me but I have not taken him. 14. Spain has produced Cervantes and Lope de Vega.

[1] Insert *in*.   [2] Translate *five hundred enemies*.

CHAPTER XXIV.

MOODS AND TENSES

The Indicative

239. The tenses of the Indicative are used in Spanish in nearly the same manner as in English. The following differences are to be observed:

240. The Present is used after **hace,** it is (*lit.* it makes), to indicate that an action begun in the past is still continuing.

Ex.—Hace mucho tiempo que la aguardo,
I have been waiting for her a long time.

Hace dos años que estamos en Nueva York,
We have been in New York two years.

Past Indefinite (Perfect)

241. The Past Indefinite is formed by adding the past participle to the present indicative of **haber: he dicho, ha llegado.**

It is used:

(1) To indicate that an action took place in the past: (*a*) at a time not definitely specified.

Ex.—Han mandado las cartas al correo,
They have sent the letters to the post-office.

He viajado mucho por España,
I have travelled much in Spain.

(*b*) At a specified time which is not completely passed. *Cf.* § **243.**

117

Ex.—Hemos visto grandes acontecimientos en este siglo, | *We have seen great events in this century.*

He recibido hoy una carta de mi padre, | *I have received to-day a letter from my father.*

(2) When the action, although passed, may take place again or is still connected with the present by its effect, results, etc.

Ex.—Las madres han sido siempre cariñosas para sus hijos, | *Mothers have always been fond of their children.*

Los Romanos han dejado monumentos admirables, | *The Romans have left admirable monuments.*

Compare with the above:

Su madre fué muy cariñosa para él, | *His (late) mother was very fond of him (ha sido here would mear that the mother has ceased to be fond of him but may be so again).*

Los Romanos hicieron grandes conquistas, | *The Romans made great conquests.*

NOTE.—Unless absolutely required, the past indefinite is often replaced by the preterit.

Imperfect Indicative

242. The Imperfect Indicative in Spanish corresponds:

(1) To the English *was* and a present participle, denoting a prolonged action in the past.

Ex.—Yo estudiaba mientras mi hermano leía, | *I was studying while my brother was reading.*

No entendía palabra de lo que decían, | *He did not understand (was not understanding) a word of what they were saying.*

(2) To the English *used to*, denoting habitual action in the past.

Ex.—Los Griegos cultivaban las artes y recompensaban el mérito,	*The Greeks used to cultivate the arts, and to reward merit.*
El verano pasado, le veía todos los días,	*Last summer I used to see him every day.*

Preterit

243. The Preterit is used when the action occurs at (or within) a definite time entirely past. (Historical past in English.)

Ex.—El buque fondeó á las tres de la tarde,	*The ship sank at three P. M.*
Le encontré el año pasado,	*I met him last year.*

244. The following examples will further illustrate the difference between the imperfect and the preterit:

Llegó mi amigo al tiempo que yo le **escribía,**	*My friend arrived when I was writing to him.*
El portero le **dijo** que un caballero le **esperaba** en su despacho,	*The janitor told him that a gentleman was waiting for him in his office.*
Mi tío me **llevó** á su casa cuando yo **era** niño y se **encargó** de mi educación,	*My uncle took me to his house when I was a child, and he took charge of my education.*

Pluperfect and Past Anterior

245. The pluperfect is formed by adding the past participle to the imperfect indicative of **haber**: **había visto, habían dicho.** The past anterior is obtained by adding the past participle to the preterit of **haber**: **hube encontrado, hubo hablado.** Both of these tenses indicate that a past action took place before another action also passed.

The difference between the two tenses is that the action expressed by the pluperfect precedes the other by an indefinite period, while the past anterior denotes an action taking place *immediately* before the other. The past anterior is always introduced by a conjunction of time like **apenas**, *hardly ;* **cuando**, *when ;* **al punto que**, *as soon as*, etc., and followed by a preterit.

Compare the following:

Yo **había** leído la carta cuando llegó mi amigo,	*I had read the letter when my friend arrived.*
Cuando **hube** leído el papel, se lo devolví,	*When I had read the paper, I returned it to him.*
No tuve necesidad de despertarle porque se **había** levantado ya,	*I did not need to waken him, because he had already gotten up.*
Apenas **hube** despertado cuando me llamó el criado,	*I had hardly awakened when the servant called me.*

NOTE.—The preterit often takes the place of the past anterior :

Cuando cesó la lluvia se puso en camino,	*When the rain (had) ceased, he started on his way.*

Future

246. The future is sometimes used instead of the present to denote approximation or probability.

Ex.—¿ Qué hora es? Serán las ocho,	*What time is it ? It is about eight o'clock.*
Mi amigo no escribe, estará malo,	*My friend does not write, he is probably sick (he must be sick).*

NOTE.—When doubt is implied about a future action taking place, the future subjunctive should be used. See § **259.**

Future Anterior

247. The future anterior is obtained by adding the past participle to the future indicative of **haber: habré leído, habrá ido.** It is used to indicate that a future action will be completed before another future action takes place.

Ex.—Á las seis habré ter- | *At six o'clock I shall have finished*
minado mi trabajo y | *my work and we will be able to go*
podremos salir, | *out.*

NOTE.—The future anterior, like the future, may express an idea of approximation or possibility (see § **246**).

Ex.—No encuentro mi libro, | *I do not find my book ; I must have*
lo habré perdido, | *lost it.*

Imperative

248. The imperative is limited to the second person and can only be used in positive commands. All other persons and all negative imperatives are expressed by the present subjunctive.

Ex.—Lleva esta carta al co- | *Carry (thou) this letter to the post-*
rreo, | *office.*
Óyeme bien y no olvi- | *Hear (thou) me well and do not*
des mis palabras, | *forget my words.*
Sepa V. lo que pasa, | *Learn (you, 3d person singular)*
| *what is happening.*
Vivamos en paz con | *Let us live in peace with all men.*
todos los hombres,

EXERCISE XXIV.

A. 1. No había andado quince pasos cuando oyó una voz que gritaba cerca de él. 2. Tus padres han sido hombres de bien, sé cual ellos y vivirás dichoso. 3. Pesqué ayer todo el día y no cogí más que un pescadito. 4. Las ruinas de las antiguas ciudades nos señalan la morada de hombres que no hemos conocido. 5. El salvaje corre hacia Robinson, se humilla, besa la tierra, le toma un pie y lo pone sobre su propio cuello. 6. Las puertas se abren á las tres y empieza la función á las cuatro. 7. Luego que me hube levantado, abrí la ventana: ya había salido el sol y las aves cantaban en los árboles.

B. 1. Last winter there was much snow when I was in the country. 2. The two travelers arrived at the place where a carriage was awaiting them. 3. To-morrow we shall go to the city, and we shall buy toys for[1] the children. 4. Cervantes has left us an admirable book. 5. Let us begin our studies. 6. Thou[2] shalt honor[3] thy[2] father and thy[2] mother. 7. This poor man has begged in vain the protection of his former friends; all forgot[4] him in their[5] prosperity. 8. It is now four years since he has been in the army. 9. If we want good friends, let us choose them with prudence. 10. I met him last week and spoke to him about[6] the affair. 11. When he shall have arrived in Paris he will send me my book. 12. He wrote two or three times but he did not receive any answer.

[1] para (§ 304).   [2] Omit.   [3] Future.   [4] Reflexive.   [5] Translate the.
[6] Translate of.

CHAPTER XXV.

THE SUBJUNCTIVE *

249. The subjunctive is the mood of uncertainty. Except as specified in § **256,** it is found only in subordinate clauses.

250. When a principal clause through its meaning or form implies that the action or state expressed by a subordinate verb may or may not take place †, or have taken place, the verb of the subordinate clause is put in the subjunctive.

251. Therefore the subjunctive will be used in a subordinate clause:

(1) When the verb of the governing clause implies: *doubt, wish, command, request, fear, prohibition.*

Ex.—Dudo que **sea** culpable,   *I doubt his being guilty.*

Su padre desea que le **dé** lecciones,   *His father wants me to give him lessons.*

Mandaré al criado que **lleve** esas cartas al correo,   *I shall order the servant to carry those letters to the post-office.*

Le ruego á V. que me **otorgue** su protección,   *I beg you to grant me your protection.*

Temo que le **hable** del asunto,   *I fear he may speak to him about the affair.*

Prohibo que **salgan,**   *I forbid their going out.*

Su padre no ha permitido que él **estudiase** el derecho,   *His father did not allow him to study law.*

---

* No attempt is made to give here anything like a complete treatise of the subjunctive. Only such rules are given as may be of use to beginners.

† *Cf.* **252.**

(2) After interrogative * and negative verbs, when the possibility of the assertion contained in the subordinate clause is questioned.

Ex.—¿Cree V. que lo **haya** hecho?   *Do you believe that he has done it?*

No creo que **esté** contento,   *I do not believe that he is satisfied.*

No digo que esto **sea** verdadero,   *I do not say that this is true.*

(3) After impersonal verbs, or impersonal expressions which do not imply certainty.

Ex.—Conviene que le **ayuden,**   *It is advisable for them to help him.*

Es justo que lo **sepa,**   *It is just that he should know it.*

but : Es cierto que lo cree,   *It is certain that he believes it.*

252. The subjunctive is also required after verbs denoting an emotion (joy, surprise, grief, etc.), even though the action in the dependent clause be a certainty.

Ex.—Me alegro que no **hayan** sucedido desgracias,   *I rejoice that no accidents have happened.*

Siento mucho que V. se **haya** molestado,   *I am sorry that you should have troubled yourself.*

Me admiro que **haya** creído V. una noticia tan improbable,   *I am surprised that you should have believed a piece of news so improbable.*

253. When a subordinate clause is introduced by a conjunction or conjunctive expression, the verb is in the subjunctive only when uncertainty is implied, otherwise the indicative is used.

* In interrogations, if the depending clause refers to a future action, the future indicative is used.

Ex.: ¿Cree V. que lo hará?   *Do you believe he will do it?*

Compare the following:

Aunque **llovió** toda la maña-na, fuí á la oficina,	*Although it rained all the morning I went to the office.*
Aunque **llueva** á cántaros partiré mañana,	*Even if it should rain in torrents* I shall start to-morrow.*
Pondré la lámpara de manera que **alumbre** el cuarto,	*I shall put the lamp so that it may light up the room.*
He puesto la lámpara de manera que **alumbra** el cuarto,	*I have put the lamp so that it lights up the room.*

254. The most important of these conjunctions and conjunctive expressions are:

antes (de) que, *before.*
á menos que, *unless.*
á fin de que, *in order.*
aunque, *although, though.*
con tal que, *provided that.*
dado que, *in case.*
de modo que, *so that* (purpose).

en caso de que, *in case that.*
mientras que, *while.*
para que, *in order that.*
por ... que, *however, whatever.*
que, *so that, whether.*
siempre que, *provided that, whenever.*

sin que, *without.*

Ex.—No le prestaré á V. este libro á menos que me **prometa** devolvér-melo pronto,	*I shall not lend you this book unless you promise to return it soon.*
Se lo prestaré á V. con tal que me le **devuelva** esta tarde,	*I shall lend it to you provided you return it this afternoon.*
En caso de que yo re-**ciba** dinero hoy, pa-garé mis deudas,	*In case I receive money to-day, I shall pay my debts.*
El criado será bien pa-gado mientras **quede** en mi empleo,	*The servant shall be well paid while he remains in my employ.*

---

* *á cántaros, lit.:* jugfulls; *llover á cántaros,* to pour.

Dé estas monedas al pobre para que **pueda** comprar pan,	*Give these coins to the poor man, in order that he may buy bread.*
Por mucho que me **diga** no le creeré,	*Whatever he may say, I shall not believe him.*

255. When a subordinate clause is introduced by a relative pronoun*, the verb is put in the subjunctive if there is uncertainty as to the action's taking place. This is generally the case when the antecedent refers to an indefinite noun.

Ex.—Quiero un criado que **hable** español,	*I want a servant who speaks Spanish.*
but : Tengo un criado que **habla** inglés,	*I have a servant who speaks English.*
Enséñeme V. un camino que **salga** para Toledo,	*Show me a road which (may lead) leads to Toledo.*
Enséñeme V. el † camino que **sale** para Toledo,	*Show me the road which leads to Toledo.*
Quienquiera que lo diga se equivoca,	*Whoever says it, is mistaken.*

Subjunctive in Independent Clauses

256. The subjunctive in independent or principal clauses is used :

(1) As a substitute for the imperative (§ **248**). In the 3d person, it is usually preceded by **que**.

Ex.—Que se defiendan,	*Let them defend themselves.*
Que no salga nadie,	*Let no one go out.*
Vamos ‡ al teatro,	*Let us go to the theater.*

* also by a relative adverb of time.

† Note the change of article.

‡ for *vayamos*, § **207**.

(2) In optative sentences.

Ex.—¡Viva la República! *Long live the Republic!*
 ¡Séale la tierra leve! *May the earth rest lightly upon him.*
 Vaya V. con Dios, *Good-bye. (God be with you.)*

(3) After the expression **ojalá*** (from the arabic, *"Allah grant that . . ."*).

 ¡Ojalá sea verdad! *Heaven grant that it be true!*
 ¡Ojalá que suceda así! *O, that it may happen thus!*

Use of the Tenses of the Subjunctive

257. The tense of the verb in the subordinate clause is generally determined by the tense of the governing verb. If the verb in the governing clause is present or future indicative, the depending verb is:

(*a*) Present subjunctive, when it refers to present or future action.

Ex.—Deseo que esté contento, *I wish him to be contented.*
 Le aconsejaré que estu- *I shall advise him to study Spanish.*
 die el español,

(*b*) Past subjunctive (present subjunctive of **haber** and past participle) when it refers to an action completed before the time indicated by the governing verb.

Ex.—No creo que lo haya *I do not believe that he has said it.*
 dicho,
 Le prestaré á V. el libro *I will lend you this book when I*
 cuando lo haya leído *have read it myself.*
 yo mismo,

258. When the verb of the governing clause is a past tense of the indicative or a conditional, the depending verb is:

(*a*) Imperfect subjunctive (either form), if the action takes place at the same time as, or after, that of the governing verb.

---

* *Cf.* Latin : *Utinam.*

Ex.—Le aconsejaba que buscara (*or* buscase) un empleo,	*He advised him to look for employment.*
Le había mandado que estudiase (*or* estudiara),	*He had ordered him to study.*
Yo haría que obedeciesen,	*I should make them obey.*

(*b*) Pluperfect subjunctive (imperfect subjunctive of **haber** —either form—and past participle) if the action in the depending clause takes place before that of the governing verb.

Ex.—Era dudoso que por allí hubiese pasado un ejército,	*It was doubtful if an army had passed by there.*
Temía que el mensajero hubiese (*or* hubiera) encontrado dificultades,	*He feared that the messenger had met with difficulties.*

Note.—For the use of the imperfect subjunctive, in conditional phrases see § **264.**

259. The future subjunctive is found only after a conjunction, a relative pronoun or an adverb. It indicates that a future action may or may not take place, and is generally used in connection with a future indicative or an imperative.

Ex.—Él hablará cuando se lo **mandare,**	*He will speak whenever I (shall) tell him to.*
Házlo si **pudieres,**	*Do it, if thou art (shalt be) able.*
El que **trabajare** será recompensado,	*He who works will be rewarded.*

260. The future anterior of the subjunctive (future subjunctive of **haber** and past participle) is used in the same manner as the future subjunctive. It indicates that the doubtful future action may be completed before another future action takes place.

Ex.—Luego que yo **hubiere**   *When I shall have written the letter*
    escrito la carta la   (*I may not write it*), *I shall send*
    mandaré al correo,   *it to the post-office.*

NOTE.—In conversation, the future and future anterior of the subjunctive are now seldom used. Their place is taken by the present and past subjunctive respectively. This substitution, however, is not allowed after the conjunction **si**. In above examples **mande, trabaje, haya escrito** could be used instead of **mandare, trabajare, hubiere escrito**; but: **puedes** for **pudieres**.

EXERCISE XXV.

A. 1. La tierra sólo pide al hombre que labre y cultive las plantas para colmarle de sus dones. 2. Quiero que él venza á sus enemigos como hombre de honor. 3. Acerquémonos; es imposible que oigamos á esa distancia. 4. No hay posición tan humilde que no nos permita ser un bienhechor en la causa de la verdad. 5. ¿Me dispensará V. que le haga una pregunta? 6. No creía que en esta ciudad hubiese monumentos tan admirables. 7. Antes que llegue su amigo de V., le diré algo que le importa. 8. No le falta tiempo para que se justifique. 9. Poco dinero nos quedará cuando hayamos pagado nuestras deudas. 10. No tomes nunca lo que no sea tuyo. 11. Que el que tiene tejado de vidrio no tire piedras al del vecino. 12. Le mandaré á decir que me esperare (espere) dentro de pocos días. 13. Sus padres les habían mandado que se amasen. 14. Si acaso doblares la vara de la justicia no sea con el peso de la dádiva sino con el de la misericordia. (Cervántes.)

B. 1. For[1] a long[2] time men believed that the earth was flat, and it was natural for them[3] to believe it. 2. He wants

[1] por. [2] Translate *much time*. [3] Translate *that they believe it.* (Subj.)

me[1] to help him to[2] write his theme. 3. I advise him[1] to choose a good lawyer. 4. Do not tell him to[1] come. 5. The doctor ordered him[1] not to go out. 6. I do not permit the children to play[1] with fire-arms. 7. We are afraid[3] they will not arrive in time. 8. Tell him[1] to come. 9. I told him[1] to come when he wished[4], but he never[5] came. 10. However much he may earn, he will never be rich. 11. I shall not go out unless you accompany me. 12. The captain has promised a reward to the first soldier who captures a flag. 13. He ordered the servant[3] not to tell[1] any one where he had gone. 14. I put it there so that no one will see it. 15. Whether he come or not[6], I shall go. 16. Set them at liberty, provided they have been faithful to their promise. 17. I am sorry[3] he did not ask me what he needed. 18. Do not eat fruit before it is ripe. 19. His friend wanted him[1] to see the room which he had rented. 20. We will answer your questions when you speak[7] with more moderation.

---

[1] Same construction as in note 3. [2] á. [3] Insert *that*. [4] Imperfect Subjunctive. [5] See § 287. [6] no. [7] Future Subjunctive.

CHAPTER XXVI.

THE CONDITIONAL

261. The principal use of the conditional is to indicate that an action would take place if a condition expressed or implied was fulfilled.

Ex.—Mi amigo compraría la casa si tuviese dinero,	*My friend would buy the house if he had money.*
Si tuviese el libro, se lo prestaría á V.,	*If I had the book, I would lend it to you.*
Me gustaría esta casa,	*This house would suit me.*

NOTE.—After a past tense the conditional is used to express the tense which would be future if the governing verb were present.*

Ex.—Dice que lo **hará,**	*He says he will do it.*
Dijo que lo **haría,**	*He said he would do it.*
Nos asegura que **volverá** pronto,	*He assures us that he will return soon.*
Nos aseguraba que **volvería** pronto,	*He assured us that he would return soon.*

262. The clause containing the condition may precede or follow the conclusion (§ **261**, first two examples). It may also be understood (§ **261**, 3d example).

263. The clause stating the condition is usually introduced by **si**, *if*, but any expression having similar value may take the place of **si**.

* The conditional cannot be used if the governing verb requires the subjunctive.

Ex.—Favorecido por las leyes, el comercio progresaría rápidamente, Si le favoreciesen las leyes, el comercio, etc., } *Favored by the laws, the commerce would develop rapidly.*

No hablaría tanto delante de su padre, No hablaría tanto si estuviese delante, etc., } *He would not talk so much before his father.*

264. The conditional is *never* found in the clause stating the condition, but only in the conclusion. Either form of the imperfect subjunctive may be used in the clause stating the condition, but only the first imperfect subjunctive may take the place of the conditional in the conclusion.

Ex.—Si **tuviese** tiempo, yo lo **haría,**
Si **tuviera** tiempo, yo lo **haría,**
Si **tuviese** tiempo, yo lo **hiciera,**
Si **tuviera** tiempo, yo lo **hiciera,** } *If I had time, I would do it.*

NOTE.—The conditional cannot take the place of the imperfect subjunctive : **si tendría** . . . is inadmissible.

265. The conditional is also used :

(1) To denote approximation or probability, when referring to a past action (*Cf.* future indicative § **246**).

Ex.—Serían las diez de la mañana, *It must have been* (*it was about*) *ten A. M.*

Estaría malo pues no me anunció su llegada, *He was probably sick, since he did not inform me of his arrival.*

(2) In expressing a wish or polite request.

Desearía hacerle una pre-   *I should like to ask you a question.*
gunta *,

NOTE.—With **querer,** *to wish,* the subjunctive **quisiera** is generally used for the conditional **querría.** It is the usual mode of expressing a request politely.

Ex.—Quisiera visitar el pala-   *I should like to visit the palace.*
cio,

Quisiera que V. me en-   *I should like you to show me your*
señase sus mejores   *best rooms.*
cuartos,

266. The past conditional (present conditional of haber and past participle) is used in the same way as the present. It indicates that both the conditional clause and the conclusion are past.

Ex.—Si tuviese el libro, se lo   *If I had the book, I should lend it*
prestaría á V.,   *to you.*

Si hubiese tenido el libro   *If I had had the book, I should have*
se lo habría prestado   *lent it to you.*
á V.,

NOTE.—When in English, *could, should, would,* express an idea of *power, duty, will,* they are translated respectively by the conditional of **poder, deber, querer.**

EXERCISE XXVI.

A. 1. Me ha dicho que sería feliz si supiera la lengua española. 2. Si yo no me hubiera dejado engañar por ellos, no me habría comprometido en este negocio. 3. No me espantaría el diablo en persona aun cuando se me presentara en la forma de un gran saco de dinero. 4. Si el ser

---

* A condition is here understood, for instance : *si V. lo permitiese,* if you will allow it.

libre consistiera en hacer siempre lo que se quiere, nadie sería libre ó mejor dicho solamente sería libre el más fuerte ó el más diestro, lo cual no sería justo. 5. Las cuatro serían cuando llegué á casa. 6. Si hubiese sabido que le gustaban tanto esas flores, las habría guardado para V. 7. Si se tuviera miedo á todos los accidentes que pueden acometernos, no se atrevería uno á moverse de un lugar á otro. 8. Hubiera dejado yo este empleo, si me hubieran pagado todos los que me han debido.

B. 1. If I had known that he was ill, I should have gone to[1] see him. 2. I would share with him if he helped me in my speculations. 3. If he had imagined that there was so much misery, he would have given more money to the poor[2]. 4. He promised that he would give it to me. 5. I should like to[3] say a few words to you before[4] I go. 6. If he had money they would not despise him so much. 7. The world would not have progressed if curious persons had not existed. 8. If this house were mine I should sell it. 9. We should have gone to the fair if he had come in[5] time. 10. There would be much less danger if every one remained in his place[6]. 11. I should like to[3] go to the country. 12. If I had known that you were not at home[7] yesterday, I should not have come.

[1] á.   [2] Plural.   [3] Omit.   [4] antes de irme.   [5] á.   [6] sitio.   [7] á casa.

CHAPTER XXVII.

INFINITIVE. — PRESENT PARTICIPLE. — PAST PARTICIPLE

Infinitive

267. The infinitive may be used exactly as a noun, and when so used it is often preceded by the definite article **el**

Ex.—El cazar es buen ejer-   *To hunt is a good exercise.*
cicio,

Me cansa mucho el ca-   *Walking tires me much.*
minar,

El saber muchas lenguas   *To know many languages is always*
es siempre útil,   *useful.*

Querer es poder,   *To will is to be able. (Where there is*
   a will, there is a way.)

Hablar mucho es un   *To talk much is a bad habit.*
vicio,

Para escribir bien una   *To write a language well, it is neces-*
lengua es necesario   *sary to know the grammar.*
conocer la gramática,

268. The infinitive preceded by **al** (rarely **con**) is rendered in English by a finite verb introduced by a conjunction of time, or by a present participle preceded by *on* or *in*.

Ex.—Al ver eso se fué,   *When he saw that, he went away.*

Al entrar en el museo   *When I entered the museum, I met*
encontré á mi amigo,   *my friend.*

Al salir el sol cantaron   *When the sun rose, the birds sang.*
las aves,

Al oír las campanas, salí,   *On hearing the bells I went out.*

Con estudiar se aprende,   *In (by) studying one learns.*

NOTE.—An infinitive preceded by **á** often takes the place of a conditional clause.

Ex.—Á saber eso (si hubiese   *If he had known it, he would not*
sabido eso) no habría   *have come.*
(*or* hubiera) venido,

269. After all prepositions except **en** *, *in*, the infinitive is used in Spanish to translate the present participle in English.

Ex.—Tengo la costumbre de   *I have the habit of rising early.*
levantarme temprano,

Después de comer, lee   *After eating, he reads the paper.*
el periódico,

Antes de morir llamó á   *Before dying, he called his children.*
sus hijos,

Salió sin decir una   *He went out without saying a word.*
palabra,

For the use of prepositions governing the infinitive, see Chapter XXIX., § **310** to **313**.

270. The infinitive is sometimes used in exclamations in place of the imperative or the interrogative.

Ex.—¡ Callar !   *Hush !*
Dirigirse al secretario,   *Apply to the secretary.*
¿ Negarlo él?   *He denies it ?*
¿ Decirlo yo ?   *I say it ?*

Present Participle †

271. The present participle is always invariable. With the auxiliary **estar** it forms the progressive construction (§ **150**). The present participles of **estar**, *to be*, **ir**, *to go*, **ser**, *to be*, **venir**, *to come*, cannot be so construed, and an appropriate tense of the verb is used instead.

Ex.—*he is going*, va (*not :* está yendo).
he was coming, venía (*not :* estaba viniendo).
he is being carried to .. está llevado á .. (*not :* está estando ..)

---

* *Cf.* § **274.**
† Really : *Gerund.* See § **142**, Note 1.

272. The different tenses of **ir, andar,** *to go,* and a few other verbs are also used with the present participle, to indicate progression or continuation.

Ex.—Va (anda) cantando por las calles,   *He goes (on) singing through the streets.*

Iba creciendo el peligro,   *Danger kept increasing.*

Sigue trabajando,   *He keeps on working.*

273. When it would be difficult to determine the subject of the action expressed by the present participle, an appropriate personal pronoun is placed immediately after the present participle.

Ex.—Encontré á su hermana yendo al concierto,   *I met your sister going to the concert.*

Encontré á su hermana yendo **yo** al concierto,   *I met your sister as I was going to the concert.*

274. The present participle usually follows **en,** *in,* when that preposition signifies *after.*

Ex.—En acabando mi trabajo saldré con V.,   *When I have finished (or after finishing) my work I shall go out with you.*

En diciendo eso salió del cuarto,   *After saying that, he left the room.*

275. After **ver,** *to see;* **oír,** *to hear,* the infinitive is preferred to the present participle.

Ex.—Me vió venir,   *He saw me coming.*

Les oímos tocar el violín,   *We heard them playing the violin.*

Past Participle *

276. The past participle may be used absolutely. In such cases a present participle (or an auxiliary) is generally understood, and is to be supplied in English.

* For the agreement of past participles, see § 143.

Ex.—Vencidos los enemigos   *The enemies having been vanquished,*
    se restableció la paz,   *peace was restored.*
    Acabada la comida se   *The dinner being finished, he retired*
    retiró á su cuarto,   *to his room.*

277. When used absolutely, the past participle may be
followed by **que** and an auxiliary. The rules of agreement
already given hold good in such cases.

Ex.—Leído que hubo la   *When he had read the letter . . .*
    carta . . . ,   *(or : The letter read . . .)*
    Comprado que hube los   *When I had bought the books . . .*
    libros . . . ,   *(or : The books bought . . .)*
    Terminadas que fueron   *When the holidays were ended, they*
    las fiestas, salieron de   *set out from the city.*
    la ciudad,   *(or : The holidays ended . . .)*

278. Note the following expressions:

No es para creído,   *It is not to be believed. It is in-*
            credible.

Estas medidas no son para   *These measures are not to be pro-*
    propuestas,   *posed.*

De rendido, se acostó en el   *He was so tired that he laid himself*
    suelo,   *on the ground.*

EXERCISE XXVII.

A. 1. Al anunciar el primer pájaro la llegada del día,
desaparecieron las pesadillas de la noche. 2. Antes de leer
una historia es muy importante leer la vida del historiador.
3. El descansar después del trabajo predispone el cuerpo
para volver á* empezar. 4. Al entrar yo una tarde al cuarto
de mi padre, le ví escribir. 5. El tirano ha oprimido á su
nación en lugar de defenderla. 6. Todas las piezas de
música que hemos oído han sido compuestas por los más

* See § **310.**

célebres maestros. 7. Queriendo saberlo todo se llega á no saber nada. 8. Viendo él que yo no decía nada continuó su relación. 9. Llegado que hubieron los viajeros, buscaron una fonda. 10. El pobre huérfano se alejó llorando y á poco desapareció. 11. Aprendida la gramática se sabe el mecanismo de una lengua. 12. Cuando salí de casa estaba lloviendo.

B. 1. All those who have spoken to-day have been very eloquent. 2. Seeing the battle lost, the general ordered a retreat. 3. On hearing these words, all became sad[1]. 4. The desire for walking made him go on[2] foot to his house. 5. The first step towards[3] wisdom is to know that we are ignorant. 6. What are you doing here? I am waiting for[4] my friend. 7. Arriving late at the hotel, the travellers did not find a[5] room empty. 8. The snow keeps on falling and the wind is[6] increasing. 9. Besides not paying me, he asks me for[7] more money. 10. I have gone six miles on[2] foot and I am tired. 11. The sailors saw an object floating in the water. 12. Let us honor the memory of those who have died fighting for[8] their country.

[1] To become sad: *entristecerse.* [2] á. [3] hacia la. [4] To wait for; translate as one word. [5] Omit. [6] Translate *goes.* [7] To ask for; translate as one word (*Cf.* Ex. XX. Vocabulary). [8] por.

CHAPTER XXVIII.

ADVERBS

279. The principal adverbs in Spanish are:

(a) Adverbs of place:

abajo,	*down.*	arriba,	*up, aloft.*
aquí,	*here.*	acá,	*hither.*
allí,	*there.*	allá,	*thither.*
donde,	*where.*	enfrente,	*opposite.*
adelante,	*forwards.*	atrás,	*backwards.*
cerca,	*near.*	lejos,	*far.*
dentro,	*within.*	fuera,	*without.*

(b) Adverbs of time:

ahora, ya *,	*now.*	entonces,	*then.*
ayer,	*yesterday.*	hoy,	*to-day.*
mañana,	*to-morrow.*	siempre,	*always.*
antes,	*before.*	después,	*afterwards.*
tarde,	*late.*	temprano,	*early.*
jamás,	*ever, never.*	nunca,	*never.*

pasado mañana,	*day after to-morrow.*
anteayer,	*day before yesterday.*
anoche,	*last night.*

(c) Adverbs of manner:

así,	*thus.*	casi,	*almost.*	alto,	*loud.*
bien,	*well.*	mal,	*badly, ill.*	bajo,	*low.*

Also most adverbs in **–mente** derived from adjectives. § 280.

(d) Adverbs of quantity or degree:

mucho †,	*much.*	poco †,	*little.*
muy,	*very.*	apenas,	*scarcely.*
demasiado †,	*too much, too.*	bastante,	*enough.*
más,	*more.*	menos,	*less.*

* with *no, ya* means : no more, no longer.

† Also used as indefinite adjectives.

(e) Adverbs of affirmation and negation :

sí,	*yes.*	no,	*no.*
por cierto,	*certainly.*	sin duda,	*undoubtedly.*
ni . . . ni,	*neither . . . nor.*	tampoco,	*no . .neither, nor. . .either.*
justo,	*indeed.*	nada,	*not at all.*
		nunca, jamás,	*never.*

(f) Adverbs of doubt :

acaso, *perchance.* apenas, *hardly.*
quizá, quizás, tal vez, *perhaps.*

(g) Compound adverbs or adverbial phrases like the following :

á la moda *,	*in style, stylish.*	al punto,	*immediately.*
al momento,	*instantly.*	á la verdad,	*in truth.*
de balde,	*gratis.*	en seguida,	*at once.*
de buena gana,	*willingly.*	por supuesto,	*of course.*
de mala gana,	*unwillingly.*	á más tardar,	*at the latest.*
de golpe,	*suddenly.*	por último,	*finally.*
á ciegas,	*blindly.*	á solas,	*alone, privately.*

de cuando (*or* de vez) en cuando, *from time to time.*

280. Adverbs are derived from most adjectives by adding the termination –**mente**, which corresponds to the English –*ly* :

(*a*) To the feminine singular of adjectives in **o** †, including the superlatives in –**ísimo.**

Ex.—nuevo, *new*, nueva.   nuevamente, *newly.*
franco, *frank*, franca.   francamente, *frankly.*
rico, *rich*, riquísimo, ri-   riquísimamente, *very richly.*
quísima.

(*b*) To the singular of adjectives which do not change in the feminine.

* And with *moda* understood : *á la Francesa,* French style.
† *lleno,* full, gives *plenamente,* fully.

Ex.—prudente (*m.* and *f.*),   prudentemente, *prudently.*
     prudent.
     útil (*m.* and *f.*), *useful.*   útilmente, *usefully.*

REMARK.—Adjectives not included in the above classification do not admit the addition of –mente.   An equivalent is obtained by using the expression : **de una manera,** *in a manner,* with the adjective.

Ex.—holgazán, *idle, lazy.*   de una manera holgazana, *idly, lazily.*

281. For the sake of euphony or variety, especially with long adjectives and those ending in –**ente, con** (*with*) and a noun, or **de una manera** and an adjective, take the place of the adverb in –**mente.**

Ex.—prudente, *prudent.*   prudentemente, con prudencia, de una manera prudente, *prudently.*
     elocuente, *eloquent.*   elocuentemente, con elocuencia, de una manera elocuente, *eloquently.*

282. The addition of –**mente** does not in any way modify the accentuation (written or spoken) of the adjective.   Both the adjective and –**mente** retain their accent.

Ex.—fácil, *easy.*   fácilmente, *easily ;* pronounced : fácil–men'te.
     perfecto, *perfect.*   perfectamente, *perfectly* ; pronounced : perfec'ta–men'te.

283. When two or more adverbs in –**mente** follow one another and modify the same word, the termination –**mente** is suppressed in all but the last.

Ex.—César escribió clara, con-   *Cesar wrote clearly, concisely and*
     cisa y elegantemente,   *elegantly.*
     Habló tan sabia como   *He spoke as wisely as elegantly.*
     elegantemente,

NOTE.—If the adverbs do not modify the same word, the

repetition of –**mente** can be avoided by using an equivalent (§ 281).

Ex.—Lee constantemente y es-   *He reads constantly and writes cor-*
      cribe con corrección,   *rectly.*

284. Adverbs are compared like adjectives (see § 52—65). The following have an independent comparison :

mucho, *much.*   más, *more.*   (lo) más, *the most.*
              muchísimo, *very much.*

poco, *little.*   menos, *less.*   (lo) menos, *the least.*
              poquísimo, *very little.*

bien, *well.*   mejor, *better***.   (lo) mejor, *the best.*

mal, *badly.*   peor, *worse.*   (lo) peor, *the worst.*
              malísimo, *very badly.*

285. Adverbs are placed before adjectives or past participles used as adjectives. They usually follow the verb, and in compound tenses the past participle.

Ex.—Es muy sabio,   *He is very wise.*
    Es un trabajo mal   *It is a work badly done.*
      hecho,
    Habla perfectamente el   *He speaks Spanish perfectly.*
      español,
    Mi amigo ha trabajado   *My friend has worked too much.*
      demasiado,

Exceptions :

(1) Interrogative adverbs begin the sentence.

Ex.—¿ Cuándo † podremos sa-   *When shall we be able to go out ?*
      lir ?
    ¿ Cómo está V. ?   *How are you ?*

(2) With the auxiliary **ser**, adverbs of quantity and manner usually precede the past participle.

---

* *más bien* means *rather*, and is not used in comparisons.

† *Cuando, cuanto, donde*, always precede the verb.

Ex.—Fué bien recompensado,   *He was well rewarded.*

Este libro es siempre   *This book is always read with*
leído con placer,   *pleasure.*

(3) Adverbs of negation (see below, § **286**).

Negation

286. The negation in Spanish is obtained by placing **no** before the verb; in compound tenses it is placed before the auxiliary. If the verb is omitted, **no** follows the word which is to be made negative.

Ex.—No llegará hoy,   *He will not arrive to-day.*

No ha acabado su tra-   *He has not finished his work.*
bajo,

Ahora no,   *Not now.*

Yo no. Él no,   *Not I, Not he.*

¿ Lo ha dicho V. ? No *,   *Have you said it ? No.*

NOTE.—Only the conjunctive personal pronouns are allowed between **no** and the verb.

Ex.—No lo creo,   *I do not believe it.*

No lo he dicho,   *I have not said it.*

287. **Ni, ni,** *neither, nor;* **nunca,** *never;* **jamás,** *never* (see note below), require **no** when used after the verb, but not when they precede it.

Ex.—No tengo ni padre ni
madre,   } *I have neither father nor mother.*
Ni padre ni madre tengo, }

No habló nunca de ellos, } *He never spoke of them.*
Nunca habló de ellos, }

No le he visto jamás, } *I have never seen him.*
Jamás le he visto, }

---

* *no*, no, and *sí*, yes, are often preceded by *que : digo que no (que sí)*, I say no (yes).

NOTE.—**Jamás** and **nunca** have sometimes the meaning of *ever*, when used after a verb without **no**. Used alone they commonly mean *never*.

Ex.—¿ Ha visto V. jamás tal cosa ?	*Have you ever seen such a thing ?*
Hoy está peor que nunca,	*To-day he is worse than ever.*
¿ Cuándo volverá V. ?	*When will you return ?*
Jamás, Nunca, Nunca jamás (*emphatic*),	*Never.*

288. **Aquí, ahí, allí** are adverbs of place, indicating *rest* or *permanence* in *one* place without comparison with another; **acá, ahí, allá** indicate *motion to* a place, *transition to* or *comparison with* another place. These adverbs correspond to the demonstratives **este, ese, aquel** (§ **103**).

Rest.	Motion.		Applied to time.
aquí,	acá,	*here (near me).*	*at this moment.*
ahí,	ahí,	*there (near you).*	*at that moment.*
allí,	allá,	*there (yonder).*	*at a remote period.*

Ex.—Aquí se habla español,	*Spanish is spoken here.*
¿ Que tiene V. ahí ?	*What have you there ?*
Yo quisiera vivir en París; allí tengo muchos amigos,	*I should like to live in Paris; I have many friends there.*
Venga V. acá,	*Come here.*
Va ahí,	*He is going there (near you).*
Vamos allá,	*Let us go there.*
Por acá no es buena la cosecha,	*Here the harvest is not good (as compared with other places).*
Allá en Cuba, es muy agradable el invierno,	*There in Cuba, the winter is very pleasant (compared with this or another place).*

289. **Muy**, *very*, qualifies adjectives, adverbs, and past participles conjugated with **ser** or **estar**.

Ex.—Es muy contento,   *He is very contented.*
     muy bueno,   *very good.*
     muy bien,   *very well.*
     Un rey tiránico es muy   *A tyrannical king is much hated*
       aborrecido de sus   *by his subjects.*
       súbditos,
     La tierra no está muy   *The land is not much cultivated.*
       cultivada,

290. Mucho, *much,* qualifies the comparatives of adverbs and adjectives*, verbs, and past participles conjugated with **haber.** It is also used alone in the sense of *very.*

Ex.—mucho más corto,   *much shorter.*
     mucho más lejos,   *much farther.*
     Eso no me gusta mucho, *This does not please me much.*
     Ha padecido mucho,   *He has suffered much.*
     Fueron aplaudidos pero *They were applauded, but not much.*
       no mucho,
     ¿Escribe bien? Mucho,   *Does he write well?   Very.*

NOTE.—*Very much* is **muchísimo; muy mucho** is found, however, in old Spanish.

291. Dónde † or **en dónde,** *where,* indicates *rest* in one place; **á dónde,** *motion to* a place; **de dónde,** *origin* or *motion from* a place.

Ex.—¿Dónde vive V.? *or:* *Where do you live?*
     ¿En dónde vive V.?
     ¿Á dónde va V.?   *Where are you going?*
     ¿De dónde viene V.? *Where do you come from?*

292. Tampoco, *neither, not . . . either,* requires a **no** (or **ni**) when it follows the verb, but not when it precedes.

* Except the irregular comparatives of adjectives: *mayor, menor, mejor, peor.*

† *Donde* as a relative does not have the written accent (§ **121**).

Ex.—No haré eso y él no lo hará tampoco,	*I shall not do that and he will not do it either.*
Tampoco lo quiero yo,	*Nor do I want it.*
Ni yo tampoco,	*Nor I either.*

293. Recientemente, *recently*, before a past participle is shortened to **recién**.

Ex.—el recién llegado,	*the newly-arrived person.*
un país recién poblado,	*a country recently populated.*
but : Ha llegado recientemente.	*He arrived recently.*

EXERCISE XXVIII.

A. 1. Cuando yo iba á la escuela soñaba siempre con (*of*) el día de fiesta en que no iría. 2. El teatro se ha abierto hoy por primera vez. 3. La redondez de la tierra es clara y evidentemente demostrada. 4. Nunca jamás me volveré á* embarcar, he padecido demasiado en mi último viaje. 5. El recién venido le miraba fijamente, sonriendo de un modo desagradable. 6. Se reía de tan buena gana que los otros se reían de verle. 7. No hay cosa absolutamente perfecta en la naturaleza humana. 8. Apenas hubimos llegado cuando estalló la tempestad. 9. Nunca he sabido tal cosa. 10. No descansa ni de día ni de noche. 11. Trabaja mucho más inteligentemente (con mucha más inteligencia) que su compañero. 12. Ayer mi hermano tenía este libro ; hoy ya no lo tiene.

B. 1. I sustained myself constantly and energetically in the same position. 2. Remain here, while[1] I go there. 3. We have spoken very clearly. 4. Where were you going when I met you ? I was coming from the theater. 5. It is

* See § **312.**
[1] mientras que.

not too early to[2] start.   6. I will never say it.   7. This
work is very badly done.   8. While[1] you were[3] looking for[4]
happiness by[5] land and sea, I was living quietly at home.
9. The situation could be neither more comical nor more
dramatic.   10. Let us walk more rapidly or we shall be late,
and that would be worse than not to[6] have been there at[7]
all.   11. He used to speak cheerfully and courteously but
now he has changed very much.   12. He will arrive to-
morrow if not to-day.   13. Above[8] and below all the seats
were occupied, and many had to[9] stand outside the[6] house[6],
some here, some there, and others so far off that they heard
nothing.   14. He knows how[6] to[6] play although not much.

[1] mientras que.   [2] para.   [3] Use *to go*.   Translate *to look for* by one
word.   [5] por.   [6] Omit.   [7] del.   [8] arriba y abajo.   [9] See § **146**, note.

CHAPTER XXIX.

PREPOSITIONS

294. The simple prepositions in Spanish are :

á,	*to, at.*	hacia,	*towards.*
ante,	*before (an authority).*	hasta,	*till, until, up to.*
bajo,	*under.*	mediante,	*by means of.*
con,	*with.*	para,	*for, § 304.*
contra,	*against.*	por,	*for, by, § 306.*
de,	*of, from.*	salvo,	*except, save.*
desde,	*from, since.*	según,	*according to.*
durante,	*during.*	sin,	*without.*
en,	*in, into, at, on.*	so,	*under.*
entre,	*among, between.*	sobre,	*on, about.*
excepto,	*except.*	tras,	*after (immediately following).*

295. Prepositional phrases are composed of adverbs or adverbial phrases and prepositions. The most common are :

antes de,	*before (time or order).*	acerca de,	*about, concerning.*
después de,	*after " "*	además de,	*besides.*
delante de,	*before (place).*	á pesar de,	*in spite of.*
detrás de,	*behind "*	conforme á,	*according to.*
debajo de,	*under.*	en vez de,	*instead of.*
encima de,	*over, on.*	frente á,	*opposite to.*
dentro de,	*within.*	junto á,	*close to.*
fuera de,	*outside of.*	sin embargo de,	*notwithstanding.*

Á

296. The preposition **á** in Spanish is generally the equivalent of the English prepositions *to* and *at*.

Ex.—Voy á la tienda,	*I am going to the store.*
Iremos á España,	*We shall go to Spain.*
Le llegaba el agua á la boca,	*The water reached up to his mouth.*
Llegó á las doce,	*He arrived at twelve o'clock.*
de las seis á las ocho,	*from six to eight o'clock.*
sentarse á la mesa,	*to sit at the table.*
á dos pesos el metro,	*at two dollars a yard (meter).*
á diez pasos,	*at ten paces.*

297. The preposition **á** is further used :

(*a*) Before the dative and the personal accusative (§§ **234** to **239**).

(*b*) To indicate *distribution*.

Ex.—uno á uno,	*one by one.*
poco á poco,	*little by little.*

(*c*) To denote *manner, means*.

Ex.—á pie, á caballo,	*on foot, on horseback.*
Le mató á golpes,	*He killed him with blows.*

(*d*) After verbs involving the notion of *depriving, taking away* (latin ablative).

Ex.—Quitaron **al** viajero todo su dinero,	*They took all the money from the traveller.*

298. In certain expressions which cannot be conveniently classified, **á** is the equivalent of the English *on, in, like*.

Ex.—á bordo del vapor,	*on board the steamer.*
á causa de,	*on account of.*
al recibo de la carta,	*on the receipt of the letter.*
oler á rosas,	*to smell like roses.*
saber á limón,	*to taste like lemon.*

De

299. **De** corresponds usually to the English *of* or *from*, and also to the possessive case.

Ex.—Hay un poco de todo,	*There is a little of everything.*
Viene de Europa,	*He comes from Europe.*
Escribió de las diez á las doce,	*He wrote from ten to twelve.*
la casa de mi tío,	*my uncle's house.*
uno de sus amigos,	*one of his friends* (*a friend of his*).

300. De is also used in Spanish:

(*a*) Between two nouns, when the second indicates the material of which the first is made.

Ex.—una estatua de mármol blanco,	*a statue of white marble.*
un reloj de oro,	*a gold watch.*
sombrero de paja,	*straw hat.*

(*b*) Between two nouns, when the first represents an object or a person, and the second describes a distinguishing feature of the first.

Ex.—armas de fuego,	*firearms.*
un molino de viento,	*a windmill.*
un coche de cuatro ruedas,	*a four-wheeled carriage.*
un buzón de correos,	*a mail box.*
un buque de vela,	*a sailboat.*
una máquina de baja presión,	*a low pressure engine.*
el hombre de la barba,	*the man with the beard.*
la niña de los ojos azules,	*the girl with the blue eyes.*

(*c*) Between a noun and an infinitive, the latter indicating the use for which the former is intended.

Ex.—una caña de pescar,	*a fishing rod.*
una máquina de coser,	*a sewing machine.*
sala de comer *,	*dining-room.*
cuarto de dormir,	*sleeping-room.*

* also: *el comedor*, the dining-room (eating-room).

301. De is further used :

(*a*) To denote the agent of a passive verb which does not imply direct physical action (*Cf.* **por**, § **306**).

Ex.—Este niño es amado **de**   *This child is loved by his parents.*
     sus padres,
     El rey fué odiado **de** sus   *The king was hated by his subjects.*
     súbditos,

(*b*) To indicate the cause of an action or condition.

Ex.—Lo hizo **de** miedo,   *He did it through fear.*
     Tiembla **de** frío,   *He trembles with cold.*
     muerto **de** hambre,   *dead with hunger.*
     loco **de** alegría,   *crazed with joy.*

En

302. In addition to its ordinary meaning *in* or *into*, **en** may sometimes mean *on, upon.*

Ex.—Carlos está **en** la ciudad,   *Charles is in the city.*
     Murió **en** Roma,   *He died in Rome.*
     Penetró **en** el interior   *He penetrated into the interior of the*
     del país,   *country.*
     La comida está **en** la   *The dinner is on the table.*
     mesa,
     Ha quedado **en** el campo   *He remained on the battle-field.*
     de batalla,

Para, Por

303. Para and **por** are two prepositions, the uses of which are so much alike as to require close attention on the part of the student.

The main differences in their use are the following :

304. Para, *for*, expresses an idea of *destination* and *purpose*

Ex.—Trae una carta **para** el general, *He brings a letter for the general.*

He comprado un traje **para** mi hermano, *I have bought a suit for my brother.*

Parto **para** Italia, *I start for Italy.*

Este perro es bueno **para** la caza, *This dog is good for hunting (for the hunt).*

Lo dejaré **para** la semana que viene, *I shall leave it for next week.*

Un estante **para** libros, *A case for books (a book-case).*

305. Before an infinitive, **para** has the same value and is translated by *to, in order to.*

Ex.—Comemos **para** vivir, *We eat in order to live.*

Quiero papel **para** escribir una carta, *I want paper (in order) to write a letter.*

306. Por is the equivalent of the English *by* and *per.*

Ex.—Esta carta ha venido **por** el correo, *This letter has come by mail.*

Son protegidos **por** las leyes, *They are protected by the laws.*

España fué conquistada **por** los Moros, *Spain was conquered by the Moors.*

Gana mil pesos **por** año, *He earns $1,000 per annum.*

á cinco **por** ciento, *at five per cent.*

307. When *for* in English has the meaning of : *for the sake of, in behalf of, in exchange for, during, to fetch,* it is rendered in Spanish by **por**.

Ex.—Hágalo V. **por** mí, *Do it for me (for my sake).*

Hablo **por** mi amigo, *I speak for (in behalf of) my friend.*

Se ausentará **por** dos años, *He will be absent for (during) two years.*

Le he dado mi escopeta **por** su espada, *I have given him my shot-gun for (in exchange for) his sword.*

Vendió su casa por diez mil pesos,	*He sold his house for $10,000.*
¿ Cuánto pide V. **por** este libro ?	*How much do you ask for this book?*
Viene **por** la carta,	*He comes for (to fetch) the letter.*
Vendrá **por** mí á las tres,	*He will come for me at three o'clock.*

NOTE.—**Por** indicates also the place through which an action takes place.

Ex.—pasar **por** la calle,	*to go through the street.*
salir **por** la ventana,	*to go out through the window.*

308. Before an infinitive, both **para** and **por** may be used to denote purpose. **Para** implies certainty and means *in order to,* while **por** merely indicates the intention, without certainty as to the result. Compare the following :

Pagan **para** entrar,	*They pay to get in.*
Ofrecen dinero **por** entrar,	*They offer money to get in (but they may not get in).*
Tengo que trabajar **para** vivir,	*I have to work in order to live.*
Trabajo **por** ganar la vida,	*I work to earn a living (but I may not earn it).*
Tomo un paseo **para** distraerme,	*I take a walk to amuse myself.*
Tomo un paseo **por** distraerme,	*I take a walk to (try to) amuse myself.*

309. Note the following expressions :

estar para,	*to be about to.*
estar por,	*to be inclined to.*
Estoy para salir,	*I am on the point of going (about to go) out.*
Estoy por salir,	*I am inclined to go out.*

Prepositions before an Infinitive

310. The preposition required after a verb is usually the same whether the complement be a noun or an infinitive.

Ex.—Iremos á la ciudad,	*We shall go to the city.*
Iremos á verlos,	*We shall go to see them.*
Quiero papel para mi amigo,	*I want paper for my friend.*
Quiero papel para escribir una carta,	*I want paper to write (for writing) a letter.*

311. " To " before an infinitive is rendered in Spanish as follows :

(1) It is omitted after many transitive verbs, of which the most common are :

bastar,	*to suffice.*	oír,	*to hear.*	saber,	*to know.*
convenir,	*to suit.*	parecer,	*to seem.*	sentir,	*to feel, to hear.*
deber,	*must, ought.*	pensar,	*to think.*	servirse,	*to be pleased.*
dejar,	*to let, to allow.*	poder,	*can, to be able.*	soler,	*to be accustomed.*
desear,	*to desire.*				
dignarse,	*to deign.*	proponer,	*to propose.*	ver,	*to see.*
hacer,	*to make.*	querer,	*to wish, want.*		

Ex.—Basta mandarle una carta,	*It is sufficient to send him a letter.*
No conviene hacerlo,	*It is not suitable (wise) to do it.*
No deberíamos permanecer más tiempo aquí,	*We ought not to stay here any longer.*
Deseo hablar al portero,	*I want to speak to the janitor.*
Dígnese V. pasar adelante,	*Please go first.*
No podemos encontrarle,	*We are unable to find him.*
Queremos ver el palacio,	*We wish to see the palace.*
Sírvase V. tomar un asiento,	*Please take a seat.*

(2) After verbs of motion, also verbs of *accustoming, be-*

ginning, continuing, helping, teaching, " to " before an infinitive
is **á**.

Ex.—Voy á pasear,	*I am going to walk.*
Empezaron á cantar,	*They began to sing.*
Carlos aprende á tocar el piano,	*Charles is learning to play the piano.*
El padre enseña á leer á su hijo,	*The father teaches his son to read.*

(3) " To " is rendered by **de** :

(*a*) After verbs not included in the above, unless purpose
or motive is indicated, in which case " to " is **para** (§ **304**) or
por (§ **306**).

Ex.—Me alegro de conocerle,	*I am glad to know him (or V.).*
Trataré de hacerlo,	*I shall try to do it.*
No me acuerdo de haber leído ese libro,	*I do not remember having read that book.*
Quiere libros para leer-los,	*He wants books (in order) to read them.*
Habla por hablar,	*He talks for the sake of talking.*

(*b*) After most nouns and adjectives.

Ex.—Es tiempo de irse,	*It is time to be gone.*
Hágame V. el favor de llevarle esta tarjeta,	*Do me the favor to carry this card to him.*
bueno de comer,	*good to eat.*
un jardín fácil de cul-tivar,	*a garden easy to cultivate*

(*c*) After **ser**, *to be*, used impersonally*.

Ex.—Es de esperar,	*It is to be hoped.*

312. Note the following expressions :

acabar de,	*to have just.*
volver á,	*to . . . again.*
Ex.—Acaba de llegar,	*He has just arrived.*
Vuelve á pedir dinero,	*He asks again for money.*

* *Cf. haber de,* § **144.**

EXERCISE XXIX.

A. 1. Una noche despertó del primer sueño porque llamaban á la puerta. 2. El amigo en la adversidad es amigo en la realidad. 3. Mas viendo mi perro que no me acordaba de él, se fué al fondo del jardín y vino hacia mí trayendo en la boca una rama de miosotis. 4. Llegó Colón á Barcelona, donde se habían hecho todos los preparativos para un recibimiento solemne y magnífico. 5. La pobreza llama algunas veces en la casa del hombre laborioso pero nunca llega á entrar. 6. Por algo y para algo nos dió el Criador un alma inmortal. 7. Sé indulgente para con todos y avaro para contigo. 8. Me he visto obligado á enviar por un médico. 9. Hemos nacido para ayudarnos mutuamente. 10. Pájaro que sabe cantar y no quiere cantar, es menester hacerle cantar. 11. Me parece oír repicar las campanas. 12. La historia romanesca del Cid llegó á hacer olvidar su historia verdadera. 13. El deseo de saber es una forma de curiosidad. 14. Su mayor placer consiste en hacer bien. 15. Se pusieron á pasear delante de la casa.

B. 1. I walked[1] all night through the fields without a[2] guide and without knowing where I was; at daybreak I found myself close to some marshes far from any[3] habitation. 2. He works from nine to eleven o'clock in[4] the morning. 3. The thief was taken[5] before the judge. 4. He has arranged a bedroom for his son who arrived yesterday. 5. The man with the white hat has passed (by) here. 6. He bought that silver watch for fifteen dollars but he sold it to me for less. 7. The ancient Greeks did not build roofs for their theatres. 8. This portrait was made by a good painter. 9. I shall give him money for his journey. 10. A servant came to open the door. 11. On the

---

[1] Use *andar*. [2] Omit. [3] Translate *all*. [4] de. [5] Use *llevar*.

table there are two gold pins for you.   12. How much do
you ask for that fishing-rod?   It is worth [1] five dollars, but
I will sell it to you for three.   13. In order to please, it is
necessary [2] to be cheerful and courteous.   14. He worked all
night without finishing the work.   15. We must obey the [3]
laws.   16. To-day we cannot go out; the weather is too bad.
17. Please [4] consider the situation in which I am [5].   18. If
you wish to accompany me, I am going to take a walk.
19. Nobody can be happy without working.   20. The train
has just arrived, and it will not go out again to-day.

[1] to be worth: *valer*.   [2] *Cf. A* 10.   [3] Translate *to the laws*.   [4] Use *dignarse*.   [5] Translate *I find myself*.

CHAPTER XXX.

CONJUNCTIONS.—INTERJECTIONS

Conjunctions

313. The simple conjunctions in Spanish are:

como,	*as.*	pues,	*since, then.*
ni,	*nor, neither.*	que,	*that, than.*
ó (ú),	*or* (§ 317).	si,	*if, whether.*
pero, mas, sino,	*but* (§ 318).	y (é),	*and* (§ 316).

314. Conjunctive phrases are composed of prepositions or adverbs followed by **que**, *that.* Besides those given in § **254,** the most common are:

así que,	*so that.*	en vez de que,	*instead of.*
con que,	*so, therefore.*	hasta que,	*until.*
de modo que,	*so that.*	luego que,	*as soon as.*
desde que,	*since.*	no obstante que,	*notwithstanding.*
después que,	*after.*	porque,	*because, in order that.*
en tanto que,	*while, in case that.*	tanto que,	*so that.*

315. Correlative conjunctions are conjunctions used in pairs, the second completing the meaning of the first. The principal ones are:

apenas . . . cuando,	*scarcely . . . . when.*
así. . . . . . . como,	*both . . . . . . and.*
así como . . . así,	*just as . . . . . so.*
ni . . . . ni,	*neither . . . . . nor.*
ó . . . . ó,	*either . . . . . or.*
sea . . . . . sea,	*whether . . . . or.*
ya. . . . . . . ya,	{ *whether . . . . or,* { *sometimes . . sometimes.*

159

316. **Y,** *and,* is changed to **é** before words beginning with **i** or **hi.**

Ex.—Franceses é Ingleses,   *Frenchmen and Englishmen.*
    padre é hijo,   *father and son.*

This change does not take place before **y** or **hie–.**

Ex.—él y yo,   *he and I.*
    plata y hierro,   *silver and iron.*

317. **Ó,** *or,* is changed to **ú** before **o** or **ho.**

Ex.—siete ú ocho soldados,   *seven or eight soldiers.*
    respecto ú honor,   *respect or honor.*

318. **Pero,** *but,* and **mas,** *but,* are practically interchange-able, although **mas** is less commonly used than **pero.** **Sino,** *but,* follows a negative clause and introduces a contrasting affirmation.

Ex.—El dinero hace á los   *Money makes men rich but not happy.*
    hombres ricos, pero
    no dichosos,

    Tengo papel, pero no   *I have paper but I have no ink.*
    tengo tinta,

    No tengo un libro, sino *I have not one book but two.*
    dos,

    No es blanco, sino rojo, *It is not white, but red.*

    Quisiera salir, mas (pero) *I should like to go out but I cannot.*
    no puedo,

Interjections

319. Interjections are sounds or words used as exclamations to denote strong emotions. They vary in meaning according to the circumstances under which they are uttered.

The principal interjections are:

¡Oh! ¡Ah! *Oh! Ah!*   ¡Huy! (pain),   *Oh! Ow!*
¡Ay!   *Oh! Alas! Ah!*   ¡Puf! (aversion), *Ugh!*
¡Ha! (joy), *Ha! Eh!*   ¡Uf! (weariness), *Oh!*

¡ Hé ! (surprise, start), *Eh !*

¡ Ea ! (encouragement), *Come !*

¡ Ea, ea ! (impatience), *Come now !*

¡ Ca ! ¡ Quiá ! (denial, indignation), *Why, no !*

¡ Ojalá ! *Would that, God grant,* § 256 (3).

¡ Ola ! ¡ Hola ! (recognition, discovery), *Ah ! Oh ! Hello !*

¡ Olé ! (approbation), *Bravo !*

Also the following, used in addressing certain animals.

¡ Arre !
¡ Anda ! } *Get up !* (to draft
¡ Alza !   animals).

¡ So ! ¡ Jo ! ¡ Cho !   *Whoa !*

¡ Zape !   *Scat !*

320. Many exclamatory expressions are only used as evasions of more profane terms. Others, which are not held to be profane in Spanish, would be decidedly so in English if literally translated. They should be rendered by some appropriate expressions. For example :

¡ Caramba !
¡ Caracoles ! } *The dickens ! By*
¡ Canario !   *jingo ! etc.*

¡ Diantre !   *The deuce !*

¡ Por Dios !   *Heavens ! For goodness' sake.*

¡ Dios !   *Gracious !*

¡ Dios mío !   *Dear me !*

¡ Jesús !   *Oh heavens !*

¡ Vírgen santa ! *Bless me !*

¡ Válgame Dios ! *Bless me ! God help me !*

321. Nouns, adjectives, adverbs and imperatives of verbs are sometimes used as exclamations.

Ex.—¡ Anda ! (incredulity),   *Pshaw !*

    ¡ Calla ! ¡ Calle !   *Be silent ! Nonsense !*

    ¡ Diga !   *Say ! Do tell !*

    ¡ Al asesino !   *Murder !*

    ¡ Al ladrón !   *Stop thief !*

    ¡ Cuidado !   *Look out !*

    ¡ Fuego !   *Fire !*

    ¡ Socorro !   *Help !*

    ¡ Firme !   *Steady !*

    ¡ bravo !
    ¡ brava ! *(to a woman),* } *Bravo !*

322. Adjectives used as interjections require **de** when followed by a personal pronoun or a noun.

Ex.—¡ Pobre de mí !	*Poor me !*
¡ Necios de nosotros !	*Fools that we are !* (or *were*).
¡ Infeliz de mi hijo !	*My unhappy child !*
¡ Pobre de mi padre !	*My poor father !*

323. The interjection **¡ay!** requires **de** when used before nouns or pronouns.

| Ex.—¡ Ay de mí ! –de tí ! | *Alas for me ! –for thee !* |
| ¡ Ay de los vencidos ! | *Woe to the vanquished !* |

EXERCISE XXX.

A. 1. Los grandes descubrimientos é invenciones se deben en parte á la curiosidad. 2. Que uno ú otro venga conmigo. 3. Apenas concluyó sus estudios cuando fué elegido diputado. 4. Diviértete con tal que cumplas con tu obligación. 5. No puedo salir porque estoy malo; desde que estoy aquí no me siento bien. 6. Así como van los ríos al mar, así vamos nosotros hacia el fin de nuestra vida. 7. Aquel juez aunque severo es justo. 8. Sea Juan, sea Pedro, sea quien sea, el que haya hecho esto, ha hecho muy mal. 9. No viene sino raramente. 10. La felicidad tanto de los estados como de los particulares depende de un buen gobierno. 11. Pero . . . ; calla ! me parece que llama alguien. 12. Lo sé todo. Con que no es menester que yo lea la carta. 13. No cesaré de importunarle hasta que me haya pagado. 14. ¡ Con que, hasta luego ! (*Well ! Good bye !*)

B. 1. He speaks with candor and innocence. 2. This enterprise is great and important. 3. Children laugh and cry easily. 4. We wrote seven or eight times but obtained no answer. 5. Whether he was [1] sick or did not receive the letter, the fact is that he [2] did not come. 6. This man is poor but honest. 7. I want them to do it. 8. As soon as we entered the hall and sat down, the play [3] began. 9. I shall go with you since [4] you wish it. 10. This news is less certain than [5] it appears; I shall not believe it unless it is confirmed [6]. 11. She does not complain of you but of your brother. 12. I shall not start until I have received word [7] from him. 13. The happiness of a rich and liberal man does not consist in having riches but in spending them, and not only [8] in spending them but in spending them well. 14. Scarcely had the general arrived [9] when peace was established [6]. 15. Since [10] such is the state of things, let us try to apply some remedy. 16. My poor companion! He must have [11] perished. 17. So, let us go.

[1] subjunctive. [2] Omit. [3] *la función* (place subj. after verb). [4] *pues*. [5] See § 55, 3. [6] reflexive. [7] Translate *a letter*. [8] *sólo*. [9] *Cf. A.* 3. [10] Translate *since that such is . . .* [11] See § 247, note.

REFERENCE LIST OF IRREGULAR VERBS

This list contains no compound verbs except when the conjugation of the compound differs from that of the simple form, or when the simple form is obsolete.

Thus for **abstraer**, see **traer**; **extender**, see **tender**, etc.

Verbs indicated by a star (*) are conjugated in the sections referred to; for the others only a model is given in the section mentioned.

A

Abastecer, 163.

Aborrecer, 163.

Abuñolar, 182.

Acaecer, 163.

Acertar, 180.

Acollar, 182.

Acontecer, 163.

Acordar [1], 182.

Acornar, 182.

Acostar, 182.

Acrecentar, 180.

Adestrar, 180.

Adolecer, 163.

Adormecer, 163.

Adquirir *, 190.

Aducir, 203.

Advertir, 188.

Aforar [2], 182.

Agorar, 182.

Agradecer, 163.

Aguerrir, 192.

Alebrarse, 180.

Alentar, 180.

Almorzar, 182.

Alongar, 182.

Amanecer, 163.

Amolar, 182.

Amollecer, 163.

Amorecer, 163.

Amortecerse, 163.

Andar *, 197.

Anochecer, 163.

Apacentar, 180.

Apercollar, 182.

Apernar, 180.

Apetecer, 163.

Apostar [3], 182.

Apretar, 180.

Argüir, 195.

Arrecirse, 192.

Arrendar, 180.

Arrepentirse, 188.

Ascender, 181.

Asir [4].

Aterirse, 192.

Aterrar [5], 180.

Atestar [6], 180.

Atribuir, 195.

Avalentar, 180.

Avanecerse, 163.

Avergonzar, 182.

Azolar, 182.

B

Balbucir [7], 163.

Bendecir *, 202.

Blanquecer, 163.

Bregar, 180.

Bruñir *, 165.

Bullir *, 165.

[1] Regular when meaning *to tune* [an instrument].   [2] Regular when meaning *to gauge*.   [3] Regular when meaning *to post troops*.   [4] Present Indicative *asgo, ases*, etc. ; Present Subjunctive *asga, asgas*, etc. ; remainder regular.   [5] Regular when meaning *to terrify*.   [6] Regular when meaning *to testify*.   [7] Not used in Present Indicative and Present Subjunctive.

C

Caber *, 198.
Caer *, 199.
Calentar, 180.
Canecer, 163.
Carecer, 163.
Cegar, 180.
Ceñir, 192.
Cerner, 181.
Cerrar *, 180.
Cimentar, 180.
Circuir, 195.
Clarecer, 163.
Clocar, 182.

Cocer *, 186.
Colar, 182.
Colegir, 192.
Colgar, 182.
Comedir, 192.
Comenzar, 180.
Competir, 192.
Concebir, 192.
Concernir, 181.
Concertar, 180.
Concluir, 195.
Conducir *, 203.
Conferir, 188.

Confesar, 180.
Conocer *, 163.
Consolar, 182.
Constituir, 195.
Constreñir, 192.
Construir, 195.
Contar *, 182.
Contribuir, 195.
Convalecer, 163.
Convertir, 188.
Costar, 182.
Crecer, 163.
Creer *, 164.

D

Dar *, 200.
Decentar, 180.
Decir *, 201, 202.
Defender, 181.
Defenecer, 163.
Deferir, 188.
Degollar, 182.
Denostar, 182.
Dentar, 180.
Derrengar, 180.
Derretir, 192.
Derrocar, 182.
Derruir, 195.
Desbravecer, 163.

Descollar, 182.
Desflaquecerse, 163.
Desflocar, 182.
Deshombrecerse, 163.
Desleír, 193.
Deslendrar, 180.
Desmajolar, 182.
Desmembrar, 180.
Desollar, 182.
Desosar † ¹, 182.
Desovar †, 182.
Despedrar, 180.
Despernar, 180.
Despertar, 180.

Despezar ², 180.
Despoblar, 182.
Destruir, 195.
Desvanecer, 163.
Dezmar, 180.
Diferir, 188.
Digerir, 188.
Diluir, 195.
Discernir *, 190.
Disminuir, 195.
Divertir, 188.
Dolar, 182.
Doler, 183.
Dormir *, 189.

E

Embarbecer, 163.
Embebecer, 163.

Embellecer, 163.
Embermejecer, 163.

Embestir, 192.
Emblandecer, 163.

† Introduce *h* before the dipthong *ue*. ¹ Irregular when meaning *to remove the bones* (hueso, *bone*). ² Regular when meaning *to taper a tube*.

E

Embobecer, 163.
Embosquecer, 163.
Embrutecer, 163.
Emparentar, 180.
Empedernir, 192.
Empellar, 180.
Empequeñecer, 163.
Empezar, 180.
Emplumecer, 163.
Empobrecer, 163.
Empoltronecerse, 163.
Emporcar, 182.
Enaltecer, 163.
Enardecer, 163.
Encabellecerse, 163.
Encalvecer, 163.
Encallecer, 163.
Encandecer, 163.
Encarnecer, 163.
Encender, 181.
Encloquecer, 163.
Encomendar, 180.
Encontrar, 182.
Encorar, 182.
Encorecer, 163.
Encovar, 182.
Encrudecer, 163.
Encruelecer, 163.
Encubertar, 180.
Endentecer, 163.

Endurecer, 163.
Enfierecerse, 163.
Enfranquecer, 163.
Enfurecer, 163.
Engrandecer, 163.
Engreír, 193.
Engrosar, 182.
Engrumecerse, 163.
Engullir, 165.
Enhambrecer, 163.
Enhambrentar, 180.
Enhestar, 180.
Enlenzar, 180.
Enloquecer, 163.
Enllentecer, 163.
Enmagrecer, 163.
Enmalecer, 163.
Enmarillecerse, 163.
Enmendar, 180.
Enmollecer, 163.
Enmudecer, 163.
Ennoblecer, 163.
Ennudecer, 163.
Enorgullecer, 163.
Enrarecer, 163.
Enriquecer, 163.
Enrobustecer, 163.
Enrojecer, 163.
Enronquecer, 163.
Enroñecer, 163.

Enruinecerse, 163.
Ensalmorar, 182.
Ensandecer, 163.
Ensangrentar, 180.
Ensoberbecer, 163.
Ensordecer, 163.
Entenebrecer, 163.
Enternecer, 163.
Entigrecerse, 163.
Entontecer, 163.
Entorpecer, 163.
Entortar, 182.
Entregerir, 188.
Entristecer, 163.
Entullecer, 163.
Entumecer, 163.
Envejecer, 163.
Envilecer, 163.
Enzurdecer, 163.
Erguir, 188, 192.
Errar *, 184.
Escabullirse, 165.
Escarmentar, 180.
Establecer, 163.
Estar *, 150.
Estatuir, 195.
Estregar, 180.
Estremecer, 163.
Estreñir, 192, 165.
Excluir, 195.

F

Fallecer, 163.
Favorecer, 163.
Fenecer, 163.
Ferrar, 180.

Florecer, 163.
Fluir, 195.
Follar ¹, 182.
Fortalecer, 163.

Forzar, 182.
Fregar, 180.
Freír, 193.

¹ Regular when meaning *to shape into leaves*.

G

Gañir, 165.
Gemecer, 163.
Gemir, 188.

Gobernar, 180.
Gruir, 195.
Gruñir, 165.

Guañir, 165.
Guarecer, 163.
Guarnecer, 163.

H

Haber *, 142.
Hacendar, 180.
Hacer *, 206.
Heder, 181.
Helar, 180.
Henchir, 188.

Hender, 181.
Heñir, 188.
Herbar, 180.
Herbecer, 163.
Herir, 188.
Herrar, 180.

Hervir, 188.
Holgar, 182.
Hollar, 182.
Huir, 195.
Humedecer, 163.

I

Imbuir, 195.
Impedir, 192.
Incensar, 180.
Inferir, 188.

Infernar, 180.
Ingerir, 188.
Instituir, 195.

Instruir, 195.
Invernar, 180.
Ir *, 207.

J

Jugar, 182 (note).

L, Ll

Languidecer, 163.
Leer, 164.
Liquefacer, 206 (note).

Lobreguecer, 163.
Lucir, 163.

Luir, 195.
Llover, 183.

M

Mancornar, 182.
Manifestar, 180.
Medir, 192.
Melar, 180.
Mentar [1], 180.
Mentir, 188.

Merecer, 163.
Merendar, 180.
Moblar, 182.
Mohecer, 163.
Moler, 183.
Morder, 183.

Morir, 189.
Mostrar, 182.
Mover *, 183.
Muir, 195.
Mullir, 165.
Muñir, 165.

[1] *Comentar* and *dementar* are regular.

N

Nacer, 163.

Negrecer, 163.

Nevar, 180.

Negar, 180.

O

Obedecer, 163.

Ofrecer, 163.

Oler *, 185.

Oscurecer, 163.

Oír *, 208.

P

Pacer, 163.

Permanecer, 163.

Poder *, 209.

Padecer, 163.

Pertenecer, 163.

Podrecer, 163.

Palidecer, 163.

Pimpollecer, 163.

Poner *, 210.

Parecer, 163.

Placer, 163.

Poseer, 164.

Pedir, 192.

Plañir, 165.

Preferir, 188.

Pensar [1], 180.

Plastecer, 163.

Probar, 182.

Perder *, 181.

Plegar, 180.

Producir, 203.

Perecer, 163.

Poblar, 182.

Proveer, 164.

Q

Quebrar, 180.

Querer *, 211.

R

Raer, *like* caer, 199.

Rejuvenecer, 163.

Restregar, 180.

Rarefacer, 206 (note).

Relentecer, 163.

Restreñir, 165.

Recentar, 180.

Rendir, 192.

Retiñir, 165.

Reducir, 203.

Renovar, 182.

Retoñecer, 163.

Regar, 180.

Reñir, 192.

Robustecer, 163.

Regimentar, 180.

Repetir, 192.

Rodar, 182.

Regir, 192.

Requerir, 188.

Roer, *like* caer [2], 199.

Regoldar, 182.

Resplandecer, 163.

Rogar [3], 182.

Reír *, 193.

Restituir, 195.

[1] *Compensar, recompensar,* are regular.   [2] Has also Present Indicative *roo* or *royo;* Present Subjunctive *roa,* etc., or *roya,* etc.   [3] Compounds regular.

S

Saber *, 212.
Salir *, 214.
Salpimentar, 180.
Salpullir, 165.
Sarmentar, 180.
Sarpullir, 165.
Satisfacer, 207 (note).
Segar, 180.
Seguir, 192.

Sembrar, 180.
Sementar, 180.
Sentar, 180.
Sentir *, 188.
Ser *, 147.
Serrar, 180.
Servir *, 192.
Simenzar, 180.
Solar, 182.

Soldar, 182.
Soler ¹, 183.
Soltar, 182.
Solver, 183.
Sollar, 182.
Sonar, 182.
Soñar, 182.
Sosegar, 180.
Sustituir, 195.

T

Tallecer, 163.
Tañer, 164.
Temblar, 180.
Tender ², 181.
Tener *, 216.
Tentar ³, 180.

Teñir, 192.
Torcer, 183.
Tostar, 182.
Traducir, 203.
Traer *, 217.

Travesar, 180.
Trocar, 182.
Tronar, 182.
Tropezar, 180.
Tullir, 165.

V

Valer *, 215.
Venir *, 219.
Ventar, 180.
Ver *, 220.

Verdecer, 163.
Verter, 181.
Vestir, 192.

Volar, 182.
Volcar, 182.
Volver, 183.

Y

Yacer ⁴.

¹ Present Indicative and Imperfect Indicative only. ² *Pretender* is regular. ³ *con-*, *de-*, *in-tentar*, are regular. ⁴ Present Indicative 1st person *yazco* or *yazgo*, or *yago*, remainder regular; Present Subjunctive *yazca, yazcas*, etc. ; *yazga, yazgas*, etc. ; *yaga, yagas*, etc.

GENERAL VOCABULARIES

SPANISH-ENGLISH VOCABULARY

ABBREVIATIONS :

m., masculine.   *f.*, feminine.

A

á, to, at, in.
abogado, *m.*, lawyer.
abrir, to open.
absolut–o, (–a), absolute.
acaso, perhaps.
accidente, accident.
acercar, to approach.
acometer, to attack, to assault.
acordarse (de), to remember.
admirable, admirable.
adversidad, *f.*, adversity.
ahora, now.
alejarse, to remove further, to go away.
alhaja, *f.*, jewel.
algo, something, anything.
alguien, somebody, anybody.
alguno, some, any.
alma, *f.*, soul.
allá, there (motion).
allí, there (rest).
amar, to love.
amig–o (–a), friend.
am–o (–a), master (mistress).
anchura, *f.*, width.

andar, to go (*indef.*).
animación, *f.*, stir, animation.
animal, *m.*, animal.
antes, before, formerly.
antigu–o (–a), old, ancient.
anunciar, to announce.
apénas, scarcely, hardly.
aprender, to learn.
aquel, that.
aquí, here.
árbol, *m.*, tree.
arrepentirse, to repent.
así, so, thus, therefore.
asunto, *m.*, affair.
atrás, backwards, towards the back.
atreverse, to dare, to venture.
aun (after verb, **aún**), yet, even.
aunque, although.
autor, *m.*, author.
avar–o (–a), avaricious ; close.
ave, *f.*, bird.
ayer, yesterday.
ayudar, to help.

B

besar, to kiss.
bien, well, very.
bien, *m.*, goods, property.
bienhechor, *m.*, benefactor.
blanc–o (–a), white.

boca, *f.*, mouth.
brazo, *m.*, arm.
buen–o (–a), good.   **estar—,** to be well.
buscar, to look for, to seek.

1

C

caballero, *m.*, gentleman, sir.
caballo, *m.*, horse.
caber, to be contained, to fit.
cada, each.
caer, to fall.
café, *m.*, coffee.
callar, to keep silent.
calle, *f.*, street.
camino, *m.*, way, road.
campana, *f.*, bell.
campo, *m.*, country, field.
cantar, to sing.
capaz, capable.
capitán, *m.*, captain.
capítulo, *m.*, chapter.
car-o (–a), dear, expensive.
carta, *f.*, letter.
casa, *f.*, house.
causa, *f.*, cause.
célebre, celebrated.
cerca (de), near.
cerrar, to close.
cesar, to cease.
ciento, hundred.
ciudad, *f.*, city.
clar-o (–a), clear.
coger, to catch.
colmar, to overwhelm.
comerciante, *m.*, merchant.
¿cómo? how?
como, as, since, like.
compañero, *m.*, companion.
componer, to compose.

comprar, to buy.
comprometer, to compromise.
con, with.
concierto, *m.*, concert.
concluir, to finish.
conde, *m.*, count (a title).
conducir, to conduct.
conocer, to know (be acquainted).
consistir, to consist.
contentar, to content.
continuar, to continue.
convento, *m.*, convent.
correo, *m.*, mail, post-office.
correr, to run.
cosa, *f.*, thing.
costar, to cost.
costumbre, *f.*, custom.
creer, to believe.
Criador, *m.*, Creator.
¿cuál? who? which?
cual, such as.
cuando, when (*inter.* cuándo).
cuarto, *m.*, room.
cubrir, to cover.
cuchillo, *m.*, knife.
cuello, *m.*, neck, collar.
cuerpo, *m.*, body.
cuervo, *m.*, crow.
culpa, *f.*, blame, fault.
cultivar, to cultivate.
cumplir (con), to fulfill.
curiosidad, *f.*, curiosity.

D

dádiva, *f.*, gift, present.
dar, to give.
de, of, from; (than).
deber, to be obliged.
decir, to say, to tell.

defender, to defend.
dejar, to let, to allow, to leave.
delante (de), before.
demasiado, too, too much.
demostrar, to demonstrate.

D

dentro, within.
depender, to depend.
desagradable, disagreeable.
desaparecer, to disappear.
descansar, to rest.
descubrimiento, *m.*, discovery.
descuido, *m.*, carelessness.
desde, since (of time).
desear, to desire.
deseo, *m.*, (the) desire.
despertar, to awake.
después (de), after.
destino, *m.*, destiny.
deuda, *f.*, debt.
día, *m.*, day.

diablo, *m.*, devil, Satan.
dichos–o (–a), happy.
diestr–o (–a), skillful.
dinero, *m.*, money.
diputado, *m.*, deputy.
dirección, *f.*, direction.
disfrazarse, to disguise one's self.
dispensar, to excuse.
distancia, *f.*, distance.
divertir, to amuse.
doblar, to bend.
don, *m.*, gift.
donde, where (inter. **dónde**).
duda, *f.*, doubt.
duque, *m.*, duke.

E

elegir, to elect.
embarcar, to embark.
empezar, to begin.
empleo, *m.*, employment, place.
en, in, on.
enemigo, *m.*, enemy.
enero, *m.*, January.
enferm–o (–a), sick.
engañar, to deceive.
entender, to understand.
entrar, to enter.
enviar, to send.

escena, *f.*, scene.
escribir, to write.
escuela, *f.*, school.
español, Spanish.
espantar, to frighten.
esperar, to hope, expect, wait for
espes–o (–a), thick.
estado, *m.*, state.
estallar, to burst, to break out.
estar, to be.
estudio, *m.*, study.

F

facilidad, *f.*, facility.
faltar, to fail, to lack.
fatal, fatal.
felicidad, *f.*, happiness.
feliz, happy.
fiel, faithful.
fiesta, *f.*, fête, holiday, fair.
fij–o (–a), fixed.

filósofo, *m.*, philosopher.
fin, *m.*, end.
flor, *f.*, flower.
fonda, *f.*, hotel, inn.
fondo, *m.*, bottom, rear.
forma, *f.*, form.
frío, *m.*, (the) cold.
frí–o (–a), cold.

F

fuente, *f.*, fountain, spring.
fuera, outside.
fuerte, *m.*, fort.

fuerte, strong.
función, *f.*, function, office.
fusil, *m.*, gun.

G

gana, *f.*, desire, inclination.
gato, *m.*, cat.
gemido, *m.*, groan, moan.
general, *m.*, general (also *adj.*).
gloria, *f.*, glory.
gobierno, *m.*, government.

grande, large, great.
gritar, to cry out.
grito, *m.*, cry.
guardar, to keep, to guard.
guerra, *f.*, war.
gustar, to please.

H

haber, to have (*aux.*).
habil, skillful.
habitante, *m.* and *f.*, inhabitant.
habitar, to inhabit.
hablar, to speak.
hacer, to do, to make.
hacia, towards.
hacienda, *f.*, estate, farm.
hallar, to find.
hasta, until, even.
helar, to freeze.
herido, *m.*, the wounded.
hermano (–a), brother (sister).

hermos-o (–a), beautiful.
hijo (–a), son (daughter).
historia, *f.*, history, story.
historiador, *m.*, historian.
hombre, *m.*, man.
honor, *m.*, honor.
hora, *f.*, hour.
hoy, to-day.
huérfano (–a), *m.*, orphan.
huésped, *m.*, guest.
human-o (–a), humane.
humilde, humble.
humillar, to humble.

I

importante, important.
importar, to be worth, to matter.
importunar, to importune.
imposible, impossible.
indulgente, indulgent.
infeliz, unhappy.
inglés, English.
injuria, *f.*, injury, insult.

inmortal, immortal.
insoportable, intolerable.
instruir, to instruct.
inteligencia, intelligence.
inteligente, intelligent.
invención, *f.*, invention.
invierno, *m.*, winter.
ir, to go (*def.*).

J

jamás, never, ever.
jardín, *m.*, garden.
jerez, *m.*, sherry.
juez, *m.*, judge.

jugar, to play.
justicia, *f.*, justice.
justificar, to justify.
just–o (–a), just.

L

laborios–o (–a), laborious.
labrar, to work, to till the ground.
ladrón, *m.*, robber, thief.
leer, to read.
lengua, *f.*, language, tongue.
levantarse, to get up.
ley, *f.*, law.
libre, free.
librería, *f.*, library, book-store.

libro, *m.*, book.
licencia, *f.*, permission, license.
lisonja, *f.*, flattery.
locura, *f.*, folly.
lograr, to gain, to succeed.
lugar, *m.*, place.
luego, soon; (–que), as soon as.
luna, *f.*, moon.

Ll

llamar, to call.
llave, *f.*, key.
llegada, *f.*, arrival.

llegar, to arrive
llorar, to weep.
llover, to rain.

M

madre, *f.*, mother.
maestro, *m.*, master, teacher.
magnífic–o (–a), magnificent.
mal, badly, ill.
mal–o (–a), bad, evil, ill.
mañana, *f.*, morning.
mañana, to-morrow; (**mañana por
   la mañana**), to-morrow morning.
mandar, to order, to send.
mano, *f.*, hand.
manto, *m.*, mantle, cloak.
manzana, *f.*, apple.
mar, *m.* and *f.*, sea.
marqués, *m.*, marquis.
marinero, *m.*, sailor.
más, more.
mas, but.

matar, to kill.
mecanismo, mechanism.
médico, *m.*, doctor, physician.
medi–o (–a), half.
mejor, better.
menester, necessary.
menos, less.
mes, *m.*, month.
miedo, *m.*, fear.
milla, *f.*, mile.
minuto, *m.*, minute.
mirar, to look.
misericordia, *f.*, mercy.
mitad, *f.*, (the) half.
modo, *m.*, way, manner; (**de modo
   que**), so that.
monumento, *m.*, monument.

M

morada, *f.*, abode, dwelling.
morir, to die.
mover, to move.
mozo, *m.*, boy, waiter.
muchacho (–a), *m.*, boy (girl).
mucho, much, many.
muerto, *m.*, the dead.

mujer, *f.*, woman, wife.
música, *f.*, music.
mutual, mutual.
muy, very.
miosotis (flower), "forget-me-not."

N

nacer, to be born.
nación, *f.*, nation.
nada, nothing.
nadie, nobody.
naranja, *f.*, orange.
naturaleza, *f.*, nature.
negar, to deny.
negocio, *m.*, affair, business.
nevar, to snow.

ni, neither, nor.
nieve, *f.*, snow.
ningun–o (–a), no one, not any.
niño (–a), child, boy (girl).
no, not, no.
noche, *f.*, night.
nuestr–o (–a), our.
nuev–o (–a), new.
nunca, never.

O

ó, or, either.
obligación, *f.*, obligation, duty
obligar, to oblige.
oficial, *m.*, officer.
oír, to hear.
oler, to smell.

olvidar, to forget.
oprimir, to oppress.
orden, *f.*, order, command.
oro, *m.*, gold.
otr–o (–a), other.

P

paciencia, *f.*, patience.
padecer, to suffer.
padre, *m.*, father.
pagar, to pay.
página, *f.*, page.
país, *m.*, country, region.
pájaro, *m.*, bird.
palacio, *m.*, palace.
papel, *m.*, paper, newspaper.
para, for, in order to;—**con,** towards.

parecer, to appear, to seem.
parte, *f.*, part.
particular, *m.*, individual.
pasar, to pass, spend, happen.
pasearse, to walk.
paso, *m.*, step.
patria, *f.*, native land.
pedir, to ask (for something).
pelear, to fight.
pelota, *f.*, ball, hand-ball.

P

pensar, to think.

perder, to lose.

perfect–o (–a), perfect.

periódico, *m.*, newspaper.

permitir, to permit, to allow.

pero, but.

perro, *m.*, dog.

persona, *f.*, person.

pesadilla, *f.*, nightmare.

pescado, *m.*, fish (out of water).

pescar, to fish.

peso, *m.*, dollar, weight.

pie, *m.*, foot.

piedra, *f.*, stone.

pieza, *f.*, piece.

placer, to please.

placer, *m.*, pleasure.

planta, *f.*, plant.

plaza, *f.*, square, market-place.

pluma, *f.*, pen.

pobre, poor.

pobreza, *f.*, poverty.

poco, little, few.

poder, to be able, can, may.

poner, to put, to place.

ponerse, to become; to set.

por, by, through, along.

porqué, why.

porque, because.

posición, *f.*, position.

postrer–o (–a), last.

predisponer, to predispose.

preferir, to prefer.

pregunta, *f.*, question.

prender, to arrest, to take.

preparar, prepare.

preparativo, *m.*, preparation.

presentar, to present.

primer–o (–a), first.

primo (–a), cousin.

príncipe, *m.*, prince.

prisa, haste.

promesa, *f.*, promise.

pronto, soon, quick.

propi–o (–a), self, own.

prudente, prudent.

publicar, to publish.

puerta, *f.*, door, gate.

Q

qué, what? how!

que, that, who, which.

quedar, to remain.

querer, to want, to wish, to like.

R

rama, *f.*, branch, twig.

rar–o (–a), rare, odd.

realidad, *f.*, reality, fact.

recibimiento, *m.*, reception.

recibir, to receive.

recientemente, recently.

redondez, *f.*, roundness, circular form.

regimiento, *m.*, regiment.

reina, *f.*, queen.

reír (de), to laugh.

relación, *f.*, narration.

repicar, to chime, to ring.

república, *f.*, republic.

resignarse, to be resigned.

rey, *m.*, king.

R

ric–o (–a), rich.
Rín, *m.*, Rhine.
río, *m.*, river.

romanesc–o (–a), romantic.
ruina, *f.*, ruin.

S

saber, to know, to know how.
saco, *m.*, bag.
salir, to go out, to come out.
salvaje, *m.*, savage.
sangre, *f.*, blood.
seguir, to follow, to go on.
sentir, to hear, to perceive, to feel,
  to be sorry.
señalar, to mark, to point out.
ser, to be.
sever–o (–a), severe.
si, if, whether.
siempre, always.

sin, without.
sino, but.
sobre, on, upon, above.
sol, *m.*, sun.
solamente, only.
soldado, *m.*, soldier.
solemne, solemn, grand.
sólo, only.
sol–o (–a), single, alone.
sombrero, *m.*, hat.
sonreír, to smile.
soñar, to dream.
sueño, *m.*, dream, sleep.

T

tal, such, such a.
tan, as, so.
tant–o (–a), as much,—many; so
  much,—many.
tarde, *f.*, afternoon.
tarde, late.
teatro, *m.*, theater.
tejado, *m.*, roof.
tempestad, *f.*, storm.
tener, to have, to hold.
tiempo, *m.*, time, weather.
tienda, *f.*, shop, store.

tierra, *f.*, earth, land.
tinta, *f.*, ink.
tío (–a), uncle (aunt).
tirano, *m.*, tyrant, despotic ruler.
tirar, to pull, to throw.
todavía, yet, still.
tod–o (–a), all, the whole.
tomar, to take.
trabajar, to work.
trabajo, *m.*, work.
traer, to bring, to carry.
traidor, *m.*, traitor.

U

últim–o (–a), last, final.
unir, to join, to unite.

un–o (–a), one (*pl.*, a few).
útil, useful.

V

valer, to be worth.
valeros-o (-a), courageous.
vara, *f.*, rod, cane, yard.
vecino (-a), neighbor.
vencer, to conquer.
vender, to sell.
venir, to come.
ventana, *f.*, window.
ver, to see.
verano, *m.*, summer.
verdad, *f.*, truth.
verdader-o (-a), true.

vez, *f.*, a time.
viaje, *m.*, journey, trip.
viajero, *m.*, traveller.
vida, *f.*, life.
vidrio, *m.*, glass.
viej-o (-a), old.
vino, *m.*, wine.
vivir, to live.
volar, to fly.
volver, to return.
volver á, to—again.
voz, *f.*, voice.

Y

y, and.

ya, now (with **no** : no more, no
longer).

ENGLISH-SPANISH VOCABULARY

ABBREVIATIONS :

adj., adjective.   *adv.*, adverb.   *s.*, substantive, or noun.
m., masculine.   *f.*, feminine.   *v.*, verb.

(These are used only when there is a possibility of mistaking the part of speech to which the English word belongs.)

A dash (—) indicates the repetition of the English word.

A

about, acerca de.
above, encima (de).
accompany, acompañar.
admirable, admirable.
adversary, el adversario.
advise, aconsejar ; avisar.
affair, el asunto, el negocio.
affection, el cariño.
afraid, to be — of, temer.
after, después de.
afternoon, la tarde.
ago, (hacer §174, haber §145).
agreeable, agradable.
air, el aire.
all, tod-o (–a), **— day,** todo el día.
allow, permitir.
also, también.
although, aunque.
always, siempre.
ambuscade, la emboscada.
ancient, antiguo.

and, y ; (*before* i *or* hi), ó.
animation, la animación.
answer, *v.*, contestar á.
answer, *s.*, la respuesta.
appear, parecer.
apple, la manzana.
application, la aplicación.
apply, *v.*, aplicar ; **to — for,** solicitar.
April, abril, *m.*
army, el ejército.
arrange, arreglar.
arrival, la llegada.
arrive, llegar.
as, como ; **as . . as,** tan . . como.
ask, preguntar, pedir.   (*See Ex. XX, Note.*)
at, á, en.
author, el autor.
avenue, la avenida.
await, esperar.

B

bad, malo.
battle, la batalla.
be, (ser §147), (estar §150).
beautiful, hermoso, lindo.

because, porque.
become, ponerse.
before (time), antes, antes de ; (place), delante de.

183

B

beg, rogar ;—**for,** pedir.
begin, empezar.
believe, creer.
below, debajo de.
besides, además (de).
better, mejor.
book, el libro.
box, la caja.
boy, el muchacho, el niño.

bread, el pan.
break, *v.,* romper.
bring, traer.
broad, ancho.
brother, el hermano.
build, edificar.
but, pero, mas, sino, (§318).
buy, comprar.
by, por.

C

call, *v.,* llamar ; **to be called,** llamarse.
can, *v.,* poder.
candor, el candor.
captain, el capitán.
captivity, la cautividad.
capture, *v.,* prender.
carriage, el coche ; el carruaje.
cause, *v.,* causar.
cause, *s.,* la causa.
century, el siglo.
certain, cierto ; **to be—,** estar seguro (de que).
chair, la silla.
change, *v.,* cambiar.
chapter, el capítulo.
charitable, caritativo.
cheerful, alegre.
child, el niño, el hijo.
choose, escoger.
city, la ciudad.
clean, *adj.,* limpio.
clean, *v.,* limpiar.
clear, *adj.,* claro.
climate, el clima.
close, *v.,* cerrar.

coffee, el café.
cold, frío ; **the—,** el frío.
come, venir ;—**out,** salir ;—**back,**
    volver ;—**in,** entrar.
comfortable, cómodo.
comical, cómico.
commander, el comandante.
companion, el compañero.
complain, quejarse.
concern, *v.,* concerner.
conference, la conferencia.
confirm, confirmar.
conquer, vencer.
consider, considerar.
consist (of), consistir (en).
constant, *adj.,* constante.
contain, contener.
cool, fresco.
cost, *v.,* costar.
count, *s.,* el conde.
country, país ; (*not city*) campo ;
    native—, patria.
courage, el valor.
courteous, cortés.
cousin, el primo, la prima.
crown, *s.,* la corona.

C

cry, *v.*, llorar ; — out, gritar.
cup, la taza.

curious, curioso.
cut, *v.*, cortar.

D

danger, el peligro.
date, *s.*, la fecha.
daughter, la hija.
day, el día.
daybreak, at — , al amanecer.
dear, (*expensive*), caro ; (*beloved*), querido.
death, la muerte.
deceive, engañar.
defend, defender.
demand, *v.*, exigir, pedir.
desire, *s.*, el deseo.
desire, *v.*, desear.
despise, despreciar.
destroy, destruir.
die, *v.*, morir.

dine, comer.
dinner, la comida.
distance, la distancia.
distribute, distribuir.
do, hacer.
doctor, el médico.
dog, el perro.
dollar, el peso (*Spanish-American*) ; el duro (*Spanish*).
door, la puerta.
dramatic, dramático.
drawer, el cajon ; table — , el cajon de la mesa.
drink, *v.*, beber.
during, durante.

E

each, cada.
early, temprano.
earn, ganar.
earth, la tierra.
easy, fácil.
eat, comer.
either . . . or, ó . . . ó.
eloquent, elocuente.
empty, *adj.*, vacío.
enemy, el enemigo.
energetic, enérgico.

English, inglés.
Englishman, el inglés.
enter, entrar en.
enterprise, la empresa.
estate, la hacienda, el caudal.
evening, la noche, la tarde ; in the — , por la noche.
every, cada, todo, (§§136, 138).
evil, *s.*, lo malo.
exist, existir.
eye, el ojo.

F

fact, el hecho.
fair, *s.*, la feria, la fiesta.
faithful, fiel.

fall, *v.*, caer ; caerse.
far, lejos ; — off, lejos, muy lejos.
fear, *v.*, temer.

F

fear, *s.,* el miedo.

few, algunos, unos, pocos.

field, el campo.

fight, *v.,* pelear.

find, *v.,* hallar ; encontrar (to meet with).

finger, el dedo.

finish, *v.,* acabar, concluir, terminar.

fire, *s.,* el fuego ; —**arm,** arma de fuego.

first, primero.

fish, *s.,* el pescado ; (*in the water*), el pez.

fishing-rod, la caña de pescar.

flag, la bandera.

flat, *adj.,* plano.

flee, huir.

float, *v.,* flotar.

flower, la flor.

for, para, (§304) ; por, (§306)

forget, olvidar.

former, *adj.,* antiguo.

food, el alimento.

foot, el pie ; **on** —, á pie.

France, la Francia.

freeze, *v.,* helar.

French, francés.

Frenchman, el francés.

friend, el amigo.

fruit, (*on the tree*), el fruto ; (*picked*), la fruta.

furious, furioso.

G

garden, el jardín.

general, *s.,* el general ; *adj.,* general.

gentleman, el caballero.

girl, la niña, la muchacha.

give, dar.

glass, el vaso ; (*material*), el vidrio ; **panes of** —, los vidrios.

glory, *s.,* la gloria.

go, ir ; andar (§197, note) ;

—**down,** bajar ; — **out,** salir ; —**up,** subir.

gold, el oro.

good, bueno ; **the** —, lo bueno.

great, grande (gran).

Greek, *s.,* el griego.

guitar, la guitarra.

gun, la escopeta ; (*musket*), el fusil ; (*cannon*), el cañon.

H

habitation, la habitación.

half, la mitad ; medio.

hall, la sala.

happen, suceder ; pasar.

happiness, la felicidad.

happy, feliz.

hat, el sombrero.

have (to), haber (*aux.*) ; (*to possess*), tener.

hear, oír.

help, *v.,* ayudar.

here, aquí (*rest*) ; acá (*motion*).

hold, *v.,* tener ; (*contain*), caber.

holiday, el día festivo.

home, to go —, ir á casa ; **at** —, en casa.

honest, honrado.

honor, *v.,* honrar.

H

honor, *s.*, el honor ; la honra.
horse, el caballo.
hot, caluroso ; **to be** — (*of the weather*), hacer calor.
hotel, la fonda.
hour, la hora.

house, la casa.
how, cómo ? — **much**, cuánt–o (–a); — **many**, cuánt–os (–as).
however, sin embargo ; por . . . que.

I

ice, el hielo.
if, si.
ignorant, *adj.*, ignorante.
ill, *adj.*, enfermo.
ill, *adv.*, mal.
imagine, imaginar.
important, importante ; **to be** —, importar.

impossible, imposible.
in, en ; — **order to**, para.
increase, *v.*, aumentar.
ink, la tinta.
innocence, la inocencia.
interest, *s.*, el interés.
iron, el hierro.

J

jewel, la alhaja.
journey, el viaje.
judge, *s.*, el juez.

July, julio.
just, justo ; **to have** —, acabar de.

K

keep, guardar ; — **on**, seguir.
key, la llave.
kill, matar.
kind, la clase ; la especie.

king, el rey.
knife, el cuchillo.
know, — **how**, saber ; **to be acquainted**, conocer.

L

labor, *v.*, trabajar.
labor, *s.*, el trabajo.
land, *s.*, la tierra.
language, el idioma, la lengua.
large, grande.
last, último ; — **year**, el año pasado.
late, tarde.
laugh, *v.*, reír ; — **at**, reírse de.
law, la ley.

lawyer, el abogado.
lazy, holgazán, perezoso.
learn, aprender (á).
leave, *v.*, dejar.
lend, prestar.
less, menos.
letter, la carta ; (*of the alphabet*), la letra.
liberal, liberal.

L

little, pequeño; a — of, un poco de.
live, vivir.
long, largo.

look, v., mirar; — for, buscar.
lose, perder.
love, v., amar; querer á (*pers.*).

M

make, v., hacer.
man, el hombre.
many, much-os (-as).
marsh, el pantano.
mason, el albañil.
master (*of house*), amo; (*teacher*), maestro.
meet, encontrar.
memory, la memoria.
merchant, el comerciante.
messenger, (*courier*), el correo; el mensajero.

mile, la milla.
miser, el avariento.
misery, la miseria.
Mr., Mrs., Miss, señor, señora, señorita, (§31 note).
moderation, la moderación.
money, el dinero.
month, el mes.
more, más; no —, ya no (*verb*).
morning, la mañana.
mortal, mortal; *s.*, el mortal.
much, mucho.

N

nation, la nación.
natural, natural.
near, cerca de.
necessary, necesario; it is —, es menester, es preciso.
need, v., necesitar.
neighbor, el vecino.
neither . . . nor, ni . . . ni (§287).
never, nunca (§287).

new, nuevo.
news, la noticia; las noticias.
New York, Nueva York.
night, la noche.
nobody, nadie.
not, no.
nothing, nada.
notwithstanding, no importa.
now, ahora.

O

obey, obedecer.
object, *s.*, el objeto; (*cause*), el motivo.
obtain, obtener.
occupy, ocupar.
o'clock, hora; five —, las cinco.
officer, el oficial.

old, *adj.*, viejo; — man, el anciano, el viejo.
on, sobre; en; encima de; á.
only, sólo, únicamente.
open, v., abrir.
open, *adj.*, abierto.
opera, la ópera.

O

or, ó; (*before* o, *or* ho), ú.
orange, la naranja.
order, *v.*, mandar.
order, *s.*, la orden.

other, otro.
out, *adv.*, fuera.
oven, el horno.
overtake, alcanzar.

P

page, la página.
painter, el pintor.
palace, el palacio.
paper, el papel; news —, el periódico.
parents, los padres.
parlor, el salón; la sala.
pass, *v.*, pasar.
patience, la paciencia.
pay, *v.*, pagar.
peace, la paz.
pear, la pera.
pen, la pluma.
penknife, el cortaplumas.
perish, perecer.
permit, *v.*, permitir.
person, la persona.
Peter, Pedro.
pin, *s.*, el alfiler.
place, *v.*, colocar; poner.
place, *s.*, el sitio; el lugar; (*city*), la plaza.
play, *v.*, (*a game*), jugar; (*music*), tocar.
play, *s.*, la pieza; la función.
please, agradar; placer.

pleasure, el placer; el gusto.
pocket, *s.*, el bolsillo.
poor, *adj.*, pobre; *s.*, el pobre.
portrait, el retrato.
position, la posición.
praise, *v.*, alabar.
prefer, preferir.
prepare, preparar.
prince, el príncipe.
print, *v.*, imprimir.
probable, probable.
produce, *v.*, producir.
progress, *v.*, adelantar.
progress, *s.*, el progreso.
promise, *v.*, prometer.
promise, *s.*, la promesa.
prosperity, la prosperidad.
protect, proteger.
protection, la protección; el amparo.
proverb, el proverbio; (*the saying*), el refrán.
prudence, la prudencia.
prudent, prudente.
pursue, perseguir.
put, poner; — on, ponerse.

Q

quarrel, *v.*, reñir.
queen, la reina.

question, *s.*, la cuestión.
quiet, *adj.*, tranquilo.

R

railroad, el ferrocarril.
rain, v., llover.
rain, s., la lluvia.
rapid, rápido.
read, leer.
receive, recibir.
recommend, recomendar.
reëstablish, restablecer.
reflection, la reflexión.
relate, contar.
remain, v., permanecer; quedar.
remedy, el remedio.
remember, acordarse de.
rent, v., alquilar.
retreat, s., la retirada.

return, v., volver; (give back), devolver.
reward, s., la recompensa; el premio.
rich, rico.
riches, las riquezas.
ripe, maduro.
rise, v., (go up), subir; (get up), levantarse.
river, el río.
roguish, burlón.
roof, el tejado; el techo.
room, s., el cuarto; la habitación.
rout, v., derrotar.

S

sail, la vela; — boat, buque de vela.
sailor, el marinero.
salute, v., saludar.
same, mism-o (-a).
say, decir.
scarcely, apenas.
scold, v., reñir.
sea, s., el mar.
seamstress, la costurera.
season, la estación.
seat, s., el asiento.
see, ver.
seek, buscar.
sell, vender.
send, enviar; mandar.
servant, el criado; la criada.
serve, servir.
set, — out, salir; — at liberty, poner en libertad; (of the sun), ponerse.
Seville, Sevilla.

share, v., dividir (con); — in, participar.
sick, malo, enfermo.
siege, el sitio.
sight, la vista.
silent, to be —, callar.
silver, la plata.
since, conj., pues; prep., desde; adv., después.
sir, señor.
sister, la hermana.
sit (down), sentarse.
situation, la situación.
sleep, v., dormir.
sleep, s., el sueño.
small, pequeño.
snow, v., nevar.
snow, s., la nieve.
so, tan; (thus), así; — much, tant-o (-a); — many, tant-os (-as).
soldier, el soldado.

S

son, el hijo.
sorrow, el dolor.
sorry, to be —, sentir.
soul, el alma, *f.*
Spain, España, *f.*
Spaniard, el español.
Spanish, español.
speak, hablar.
speculation, la especulación.
spend (*money*), gastar; (*time*), pasar.
spite, in — of, á pesar de.
square la plaza.
stand, *v.*, estar de pie.

start, *v.*, partir.
state, el estado.
steamer, el vapor.
step, *s.*, el paso.
still, todavía; — more, aun más.
storm, la tempestad.
street, la calle.
study, *v.*, estudiar.
study, *s.*, el estudio.
such, tal; — a, semejante.
summer, el verano.
surprise, *v.*, sorprender.
surrender, *v.*, rendirse.
sustain, sostener.

T

table, la mesa.
take, tomar; — care, tener cuidado; — off one's hat, quitarse el sombrero; — with one's self, llevar consigo.
tell, decir; — a story, contar un cuento.
theater, el teatro.
theme, el tema.
then, entonces; (*afterwards*), luego.
there, allí (*rest*); allá (*motion*).
thief, el ladrón.
thing, la cosa.
think, pensar; creer.
through, por.
time, *s.*, el tiempo; a —, una vez; times, veces; in —, á

tiempo; what —?, ¿qué hora?
tire, *v.*, cansar.
to-day, hoy.
to-morrow, mañana.
too (*also*), también; — much, demasiado.
towards, hacia; (*mental*), para con.
town, la ciudad; la población.
toy, *s.*, el juguete.
train, *s.*, el tren.
translate, traducir.
traveller, el viajero.
tree, el árbol.
Troy, Troya.
true, verdadero; it is —, es verdad.
try, tratar.
Tuesday, el mártes.

U

uncle, el tío.
understand, entender, comprender.
United States, los Estados Unidos.

unless, á menos que.
until, hasta, hasta que.
useful, útil.
use to, soler.

V

vain, vano.

very, muy; bien.

W

wait (for), esperar.
walk, *v.,* pasear; **to take a —,**
    dar un paseo.
walk, *s.,* el paseo.
wall, la muralla.
want, *v.,* querer.
war, la guerra.
watch, *s.,* el reloj.
water, *s.,* el agua, *f.*
weather, el tiempo.
Wednesday, el miércoles.
week, la semana.
well, *adv.,* bien.
when, cuando, ¿cuándo?
whether . . . or, sea . . . sea.
while, mientras, mientras que.
white, blanco.
wind, el viento.
windy, it is —, hay (hace) viento.

window, la ventana.
wine, el vino.
winter, el invierno.
wisdom, la sabiduría.
wise, sabio.
wish, *v.,* querer; desear.
with, con.
without, sin; (*outside*), fuera.
woman, la mujer.
word, la palabra.
work, *v.,* trabajar.
work, *s.,* el trabajo; (*literary*),
    la obra.
workman, el obrero.
world, el mundo.
worse, peor.
worth, to be —, valer.
wound, *v.,* herir.
write, escribir.

Y

year, el año.
yesterday, ayer.
yet, *adv.,* todavía; **not —,** ya no,

todavía no.
young, joven; **— man,** el joven;
    — lady, la señorita.